PASSIONATE Pursuit

A Story of God's Faithfulness
ANITA PEARCE

Printed in Canada

Soft cover ISBN: 978-1-4866-2487-4
eBook ISBN: 978-1-4866-2488-1

Word Alive Press
119 De Baets Street Winnipeg, MB R2J 3R9
www.wordalivepress.ca

Cataloguing in Publication information can be obtained from Library and Archives Canada.

To Darlene Kienle,
beautiful soul, treasured friend,
one of my life's greatest blessings.

To everyone who encouraged and supported me,
welcoming me into your churches,
homes and hearts.
Thank you.

TABLE OF CONTENTS

Acknowledgements

Many people have encouraged me to write my story. They were interested in how I came to know Christ as my Savior as well as how He led me through unique ministry experiences. I'm indebted to wonderful friends and colleagues who assisted me with this project. I am deeply grateful for every encouragement and kindness.

Darlene Kienle, you have walked much of the story with me. Your enduring friendship is a valued treasure.

Karl Kienle, you insisted that my story is worth telling. Your faithfulness in God's service has an eternal reward.

Doreen Holdsworth, you helped make the story readable. It has been delightful to work with you as you willingly shared your time and talent.

Judy Shaw, you have a unique perspective from inside the story. Your listening ear and encouragement have been greatly appreciated.

Velma Henderson, you know the story from the beginning. Always my sister, forever my friend.

Alice Dutcyvich, you taught me how to write a story for publication in the first place. You and your daughter Kara's expertise on this project has been invaluable.

Board of Inspiration Ministries, you are my friends and fellow laborers, supporting me through the story.

Word Alive Press, you have given practical advice to help make this story known.

INTRODUCTION

The sky was dazzling! The reflected splendor of a million stars danced on the drifts of snow.

I stood near the mission house where I had been invited to preach in Nuuk, Greenland. The Lord's powerful presence had been at work in the services. Now, in the crisp Arctic night, I was stunned in awesome wonder. Each star, known and named by God, served His purpose to display His glory.

Like those stars, every person is also unique, embodying different capacities, resources, and personalities. No one can be like me and I can never be like anyone else. We all have an exclusive, one-of-a-kind story to tell of God's amazing grace. We have been distinctively designed to fulfill our part of God's perfect plan. Even in the remotest corners of the planet, the gospel of Christ reveals the intrinsic and eternal value of every individual to God.

This book is part of my story. Along life's journey, I have made an abundance of mistakes. That's why I am compelled to emphasize the faithfulness of God! He has been merciful to watch over me, warn of dangers, and direct me through minefields of temptation. God's love and forgiveness have been sufficient for every occasion. By His grace, I am continually growing in Christ and moving forward, triumphant in His power.

While walking along a country road one day, I reflected on God's purposes for each of us in relation to success. For some, the highest achievement consists of family and friends or fame and fortune. For others, it includes possessions, power, or prestige.

With a flash of clarity, I knew what I would consider to be the essence of supreme success. At life's end, the ultimate attainment would be to hear my Savior say, "Well done."

As I walked that country road, I wrote the lyrics to a song which express my heart's desire—to pursue Christ as He has pursued me:

> Life passes quickly as a dream,
> Like a vapor briefly seen;
> Yesterday had its joy and pain,
> Tomorrow I may lose or gain;
> Shadows crossing the stage of time,
> Only this moment is mine.
> Treasures that we now see,
> Are but fleeting vanity;

This one life will soon be past,
Only what's done for Christ will last.
I'll aim for the eternal crown,
That all my life in Him be found.

Chorus:
I'll live to win the timeless prize,
To see the favor in His eyes;
For when my life's race has been run,
I long to hear Him say, "Well done."

One

TRANSFORMING GRACE

For God so loved the world
that He gave His only begotten Son,
that whoever believes in Him should not perish
but have everlasting life.
John 3:16

I hid behind my mother as she answered the door. Living in the countryside, we didn't have visitors very often. Occasionally, neighbors would drop by for tea or to help with a farm project. Consequently, we were filled with curiosity when an unknown black and white car drove into our farmyard one summer morning. Attached to the top of the car was a large plywood sign advertising special gospel services.

The stranger driving the car was a preacher who told us that a big gospel tent had been erected in town. Bible classes for children would be held during the day. If we were interested, he would pick us up and drive us there every day.

My oldest brother, Wesley, was away in the Air Force. My dad and second brother, Allan, were out working in the fields. Velma, my sister, was eleven and I was six. Velma was a little miffed; she had other plans for the day. I was very excited about this new adventure. Mom agreed to let us go.

Attending Bible classes under the big tent was fascinating. I was impressed with the action songs, the Bible stories, and the large canvas tent gently swishing in the wind. Besides the Bible classes, we were told that church services would be held every night. Thinking it would be a novel experience, we convinced the rest of the family to go.

I had never seen anything like it! I'd never dreamed that church could be so exciting. These people were actually happy to be there. They sang heartily, clapping their hands. There was action everywhere! Being a musical family, we were intrigued by the enthusiastic singing, guitars, and accordions. When the preacher preached, he used simple illustrations, turning the Bible into a living book full of stories of real people.

We were a relatively religious family and often went to church. I understood that good people went to heaven and bad people went someplace else. However, in the tent services, even though I was a child, I could clearly understand the messages. Three points were pressed home:

- First, the fact of sin. We have broken God's laws and deserve the judgment of God. As Romans 3:23 tells us, *"all have sinned and fall short of the glory of God."*

- Second, God has provided the solution. Forgiveness is available for our sin because God gave His Son Jesus Christ to die for us. According to Romans 5:8, *"But God demonstrates His own love toward us, in that while we were still sinners, Christ died for us."*

- Third, we have a choice. We can accept Jesus as our personal Savior or reject Him. Romans 10:13 says that *"whoever calls on the name of the Lord shall be saved."*

The speakers clearly presented the gospel and the Holy Spirit brought understanding and conviction to our hearts. At the end of the sermon, we responded to the invitation for us to come forward and commit our lives to Jesus. I went up with my family, kneeling on the grass in front of the platform. I prayed a simple prayer in which I asked Jesus Christ to forgive my sins and come into my heart. With the open-hearted faith of a child, I accepted Him as my Lord and Savior.

A miracle happened. I believed; I received. I was born again. The Bible says in John 1:12, *"But as many as received Him, to them He gave the right to become children of God, to those who believe in His name…"*

When my mother was still a young wife, her parents-in-law had asked her if she was converted. She said yes, mainly because she hadn't known exactly what they meant. She considered herself a religious person and felt she was certainly as good as her in-laws.

Grandpa and Grandma Pearce lived in the same yard as my father and mother. One day Grandma came to my parents' house and said to my mother, "Grandpa wants to see you."

Going to their home, she found Grandpa sitting in the old leather rocking chair. He often spent time reading his Bible and she respected him greatly for his kind and gentle ways.

"I want to pray for you," he said. He then reached up his hand, put it on my mother's head, and prayed four words: "God, save this woman." With that, he addressed her again. "You can go now."

A few months later, he died. For years, my mother pondered what he had meant by the words of his prayer. Saved? Saved from what?

Nearly eighteen years later, she finally understood. As a result of the tent services, the entire family was converted to Christ.

When we heard about an upcoming "summer camp meeting," we didn't know what it was, but it sounded too exciting to miss! Packing ourselves into Allan's old car, we drove the two hundred kilometers to Yorkton, Saskatchewan, where a big tent had been erected on the fairgrounds.

Although I was seven years old, I had rarely been to a city. There were so many people in the world!

At the conclusion of the message each night, people came to the altar for prayer. Some gave their hearts to the Lord while others received prayer for healing. Backsliders were restored to faith.

There was a lot of preaching and discussion about receiving the baptism of the Holy Spirit. It seemed to be associated with speaking in other tongues—that is, by the inspiration of the Holy Spirit, a person speaks languages they've never learned. Jesus had commanded the disciples to wait for this gift of power: *But you shall receive power when the Holy Spirit has come upon you; and you shall be witnesses to Me in Jerusalem, and in all Judea and Samaria, and to the end of the earth*" (Acts 1:8).

The camp speakers explained what had happened when the Holy Spirit came upon the believers on the day of Pentecost. In Acts 2:4, the Bible says that *they were all filled with the Holy Spirit and began to speak with other tongues, as the Spirit gave them utterance."* Scripture also teaches that this same promise is intended for all believers today: *"For the promise is to you and to your children, and to all who are afar off, as many as the Lord our God will call"* (Acts 2:39).

On the last evening of the camp meeting, many people went forward for prayer. Sometimes they fell on the ground when the preacher laid his hands on them. They seemed to be receiving a great blessing. It was called "falling under the power."

I was totally enthralled by all the action. Not wanting to miss anything, I went up for prayer too. When the preacher prayed for me, I fell to the ground like I had seen the others do. I decided to try it again! He prayed and I fell over a second time. Every time he moved on, I resurrected, went back to where he was praying, and repeated the process.

Thinking that four times was sufficient, I decided to lie on the ground for a while and see what would happen next. I was trying to see a vision or something, I suppose, because I had heard the adults speaking of their various experiences.

It didn't take long for the pastor's wife and another lady to spot me. They knelt beside me and earnestly prayed for me to receive the baptism of the Holy Spirit.

I peeked to see exactly what was happening. One woman was gently patting my stomach while the other softly touched my face while praying in the languages of the Holy Spirit. I've since discovered that these well-meaning actions have been mockingly called "the Pentecostal massage." However, they were simply encouraging me to receive and speak in the words of the Spirit.

How can I explain it? A river—a geyser, a flood—began to flow through me. Peace, joy, and love engulfed me. In simplicity, words I didn't understand bubbled out of my mouth. The presence of the Lord washed over me.

The same power as experienced on the day of Pentecost had touched my life. I didn't understand the theology of it, but I knew something amazing had happened. I would never be the same again.

Two

DESTINY DECIDED

And He said to them, "Go into all the world
and preach the gospel to every creature."
Mark 16:15

Going to church became the most exciting activity in my world. Our services were held Friday night and Sunday afternoon. Our assembly was small, but there was great liberty of worship and the presence of the Lord knit our hearts together.

Music was in our family's genes, and our parents encouraged and supported the interest and talent we displayed. Wesley played the accordion in various dance bands. Now in his twenties, he had been deployed to Germany with the Canadian Air Force. Allan had learned the guitar and Velma was adept at the piano. They could all sing well.

It was only natural that our music should be converted from country ballads and dance hall entertainment to gospel songs. Our house was soon filled with praise and worship to the Lord.

Our pastor, Russel Richardson, encouraged everyone in the congregation to get involved. He had a great ability to motivate people, particularly youth. Allan and Velma began assisting with the music and singing during the meetings. Serving the Lord became the greatest adventure in life!

Coming home from the service one Sunday afternoon, however, I felt discouraged. I went into my bedroom and began to pray. With many tears, I told the Lord that I wanted to do something for Him too. I didn't seem to have the same capacity for music as my siblings. Although I was only about eight or nine years old, I wanted the assurance that somewhere in His plan God had a purpose for my life.

I could talk, though! Mother had said I was born talking—screaming, at least. I had been covered with eczema for the first year of my life; never having been one to suffer alone, or in silence, I had developed a fine set of lungs early on.

At school, I had already won several prizes, and a few spankings, for public speaking.

"Lord, I can't sing or play an instrument, but I can talk," I fervently prayed, tears pouring down my face.

"Please let me be a preacher. Let me travel around the world and tell many people about You. Let me be a missionary evangelist."

Deep sobs burst out of my soul. I don't know how long they lasted, but when I left my bedroom that day I knew I would travel around the world as a missionary evangelist.

Since I was going to be a preacher, I needed to practice. Who was going to listen to me? Not to worry. Dressing up in one of my brother's old suits and borrowing a necktie, I set out to find a platform. We had an empty hay rack in the pasture near the barn. Perfect. I borrowed an old microphone from my brother's reel-to-reel tape recorder.

With Bible in hand, I climbed up on the rack. Cows were moving around the barnyard. It was near milking time and crowds filled the auditorium. With much shoving and mooing, they prepared to hear the gospel.

As I started to preach, the congregation looked on with fascination. Big brown eyes stared in amazement. I shouted my text, telling the cows to repent or perish.

After a few minutes of loud and lively preaching, several of them slowly walked away. Not one convert!

During one of the summer camp meetings, the leaders announced that there would be a water baptismal service. This would be a critical step of obedience and commitment to the Lord. Several of my friends were going to be baptized.

I thought about it most of the week. Finally, while standing in the middle of the campground one day, I asked Pastor Richardson if I could be baptized too.

"How old are you?" he asked.

"Ten years old." I stood as tall as my little self could. "But I've given my heart to the Lord," I added, hoping he would be impressed.

He looked at me very seriously, then told me that he would baptize children only under certain circumstances.

"Have you received the Holy Spirit baptism?" he inquired.

I was suddenly filled with doubt. Was it really the Holy Spirit that had caused me to speak those wonderful words?

"I think so," I replied somewhat hesitantly. "I have spoken in tongues."

He noticed my confusion. "Tell you what. I'll pray for you right now. While I'm praying, you pray out loud in the words you have received."

Opening my mouth, I began to pray softly. Again, I sensed the river flowing within and those beautiful words came through my lips.

When the pastor stopped praying, he looked at me intently. "Do you realize that when you are baptized in water you are giving testimony that you intend to follow Jesus for the rest of your life?"

It was a very serious moment, but I already knew my decision. I wanted to serve Jesus, who in simple faith I had come to know and love.

He smiled. "If it's all right with your mother, I will baptize you Sunday afternoon."

Three

FARMER'S DAUGHTER

*Warm familiar scents drift softly from the
oven, and imprint forever upon our hearts
that this is home and that we are loved.*[1]
Arlene Stafford-Wilson

It was quite a surprise when I arrived in the family. My father was fifty-eight years old and my mother forty-one. I was the end of the train!

Being much younger than my brothers and sister, and not understanding their interests, I usually played alone. To share my games, I invented a whole crowd of imaginary friends. I would chat with them for hours, bossing them around and even preaching to them.

---

[1] "101 Best Country Quotes Filled with Southern Charm," *Kidadl*. October 18, 2022 (https://kidadl.com/quotes/best-country-quotes-filled-with-southern-charm).

I had a strong will, hot temper, and high energy. To get my own way, unfortunately, I developed a wicked, sarcastic tongue. Most of the time I immediately repented, with deep remorse, for my nasty words… but the damage was already done. The Lord would have a lot of work to mold and make me after His will.

In my later years, one of my relatives assured me that I hadn't really been a bad girl, just very busy!

School was enjoyable. Despite my complaints about homework, teachers, and exams, I did well in my studies and was usually near the top of the class.

Being outspoken and somewhat spoiled, I earned myself some rather unflattering nicknames. I desired to tell my classmates about the love of the Lord but felt inadequate in my Christian witness. I was keenly aware of my failures.

One Sunday shortly after my twelfth birthday, however, a visiting evangelist was preaching at church. Suddenly he stopped, pointed at me, and said that he had a word from the Lord for me. With great precision, he described the call God had placed in my heart. With other words of encouragement, he confirmed the direction God had chosen for my life.

During Christmas and Easter vacations, the church in Yorkton held special events which attracted many, young people and adults alike, for times of spiritual refreshing. At one of these rallies, the preacher gave a strong appeal for deeper commitment to Christ. My heartfelt response produced a new level of surrender to the Lord. I was set aflame with passion for Christ.

Although music was an important part of our family, I lacked the discipline to learn an instrument. However, I eventually decided to learn the guitar when other young people began to play their instruments at church. To my amazement, I discovered that I had musical ability as well! In four months, I was playing with the other musicians.

I loved farm life and the great outdoors. Every season had its joys and challenges. Winter meant bringing in the wood and building snow forts. Occasionally we went skating on a pond. In the spring, we had newborn calves, melting snow, and the smell of earth and green grass. The long, warm days of summer were filled with garden work and making hay. I didn't do much of the work, to be honest, but I had fun watching everyone else!

Then it would be harvest time. Everyone drew great excitement and satisfaction from watching the grain tumble from the combine into the trucks and finally the granaries. The yellow harvest moon would add her light as the men worked late into the darkness. A hint of frost lingered in the air. High above we'd hear geese honking their way south for the winter.

Saskatchewan is described as the land of living skies, due to the province's beautiful sunsets and northern lights. It's also known for its vast fields of grain, pastures with cattle, potash mines, and oil wells. At one time, grain elevators dotted the prairie. The great expanses of open, rolling countryside gave the impression of tranquility and solitude, belying our bustling rural lifestyle.

When my sister Velma finished high school, she left for business college, and later for Bible school. As a gifted speaker and musician, she was invited to pastor a church in Ontario where she met her husband and raised her family. To this day, she continues on the pastoral staff of this thriving assembly. My brother Allan remained on the farm with the plan to eventually take ownership of it.

A widow in our church, Mrs. Wood, had a son who was the same age as me. She had difficulty finding a suitable home for him when she went away for work and my mother and father agreed to take him into our home. Subsequently, Raymond Wood became like another brother to me. Together we had many adventures.

Raymond was a patient, pleasant-natured lad who usually let me boss him about. One spring, we put our hand to building a canoe out of some scraps of wood and tin. I insisted on doing it my way and took the boat on its maiden voyage across the spring pond. Promptly, I was dumped into the icy water—and got thoroughly soaked, much to Raymond's glee! He laughed and I chased him all the way to the house.

Although my father didn't make a strong public confession of his faith, he certainly lived it. Having seen the devastation caused by alcohol, he did everything to prevent our exposure to it.

On one occasion, an uncle who was visiting from Ontario purchased some liquor. He invited his friends and traveling companions to tank up with the drinks he had brought in the trunk of his car, which he parked in front of our house. It was a mistake he would not repeat. My father roared out of the house. In no uncertain terms, he told this uncle to pack up his booze and get it off the property!

Dad also refused to get a television, convinced that it was a waste of time and money. I am so grateful now for his insight and wisdom.

We created our own amusement using our imaginations. I spent entire summer days riding my horse, exploring the hills and valleys of our family farm. We invested our time in dozens of profitable activities. The evenings were filled with music as our family gathered to play our instruments and sing together.

Very subtly at first, I became aware of my father's failing memory. However, I was too immature to realize the tragedy he and my mother were experiencing. Slowly and insidiously, he was stolen from us. Someone has appropriately named dementia and Alzheimer's disease "the long goodbye." I was eighteen the first time he didn't know me as his daughter. It was a difficult, painful moment.

Four

Bible Training

*Be diligent to present yourself approved
to God, a worker who does not need to be
ashamed, rightly dividing the word of truth.*
2 Timothy 2:15

Each summer, Pastor Richardson organized and sent three or four evangelistic teams to minister in various small prairie towns. Either he or other senior leaders, together with three or four youth, set up a gospel tent in each place.

Immediately after high school graduation, I left home to be a part of this endeavor. During the day we were involved in children's ministry, and evangelistic services each evening. It was a tremendous way both to preach the gospel and motivate young people to serve the Lord. Numerous folks were touched by the Holy Spirit.

As a result of those outreaches, several churches were planted throughout rural Saskatchewan.

The central church in Yorkton also established a training center. Classes ran from the beginning of November to the end of February. The students studied Bible courses during the day, then participated in services in surrounding towns and affiliated assemblies at night. This provided many opportunities for practical experience and training.

There was a strong emphasis on Scripture memorization. We learned reams of passages. This discipline has proved a tremendous blessing, and it's a practice I continue to this day. The verses I learned in my youth have been deeply embedded in my soul, bringing wisdom, guidance, and conviction. As the psalmist declared, *"Your word I have hidden in my heart, that I might not sin against You"* (Psalm 119:11).

I was quickly invited to sing and speak, assisting in the various churches under the pastor's care. Although I found it challenging to prepare messages, I greatly enjoyed being able to expound scriptural truth. I made up for my lack of theological depth with an abundance of energy and enthusiasm!

In my first season at the training center, I came to the painful awareness of how strong-willed and self-centered I had become. In clashes with my teachers and fellow students, I discovered deep personality deficiencies and character flaws. I continuously found myself in trouble with others, and it usually had something to do with my mouth! I had never recognized or been challenged in these areas before.

After yet another confrontation, my friend quipped, "Anita, when your ship comes in, you'll probably be at the airport!"

Thus began the serious business of letting the Lord remake my patterns of thinking, a process similar to peeling an onion; layer after layer has to be removed in what is often a tearful process. The Lord's faithfulness continually sent circumstances and individuals to encourage me as well as to confront, bringing correction and growth.

After a couple of years of study, discipline, and development at the training center, Pastor Richardson sent me to speak in other local churches. Within a short time, I was given invitations to share in assemblies in other cities and provinces, even in the United States.

On one of my first speaking tours, I had to travel alone for three weeks. For the first time in my life, I encountered opposition from those who didn't agree with the notion of women in ministry. I had never experienced this challenge before. My circle of fellowship had always been warm and accepting of women in preaching and leadership roles.

Devastated, I cried out to the Lord. What should I do? Was it all over? What about His call in my heart?

Alone in the hotel room one day, I became aware of the Lord's presence. His peace began to flow over my soul. Very clearly in my heart I heard the words of an old gospel song:

> Fear thou not, for I'll be with thee,
> I will still thy pilot be;
> Never mind the tossing billows,
> Take My hand and trust in Me.[2]

In July 1975, arrangements were made for me to make a short-term mission trip to Spain. It was my first transatlantic flight and exposure to on-field foreign missions. In one month, I learned so much by working side by side with these veteran Christian workers.

While there, I met Marguerette Mitchell from New Brunswick, a close friend of the missionaries with whom we stayed. Although she was twenty years my senior, we became fast friends. She also made arrangements with her pastor, Phil Anderson, for me to minister in their church in the Maritimes the following spring.

These invitations and connections opened doors for services in several churches in the Toronto area. I was scarcely twenty-two years old, full of enthusiasm and a desire to serve the Lord. I listened and learned much from the seasoned pastors and church leaders around me. They

[2] Emily D. Wilson, "I Will Pilot Thee," 1927

were kind and patient, recognizing my youthful zeal. They all have become lifelong friends.

Traveling by bus, I went preaching and singing from place to place, continuing on my way to the Maritimes in eastern Canada. Finally I arrived in St. Andrews, New Brunswick, where it was a joy to reconnect with my friend.

Five

HOPE IN TRAGEDY

*Peace I leave with you, My peace I give to
you; not as the world gives do I give to you.
Let not your heart be troubled,
neither let it be afraid.*
John 14:27

The first service in St. Andrews took place on the
evening of Friday, June 11, 1976. The following
day, my friends invited me to do some sightseeing in
Fredericton. We returned in the middle of the afternoon
to the ringing of the telephone. The call came from my
sister and her first words were firm.

"Are you sitting down?" With a steady voice, she spoke
the unthinkable. "Our brother Allan was shot and killed
this morning."

It was a terrific shock! Time seemed to stand still as a thousand questions tumbled through my mind. How had it happened? Who had done it? Why? What about his wife and babies? What about my mother and father? What about the farm?

My friends held me in their arms as I tried to focus. Then they rushed me back to Fredericton to catch a flight home.

It would take months, but gradually we got some answers. Two men, who several hours before had escaped from prison near Winnipeg, had stolen a motorcycle in my hometown of Moosomin. Shortly after 7:00 that fateful morning, they had traveled along the rural road passing our farm. My parents were just getting dressed when the men entered the farmyard. They walked into the house. No one locked their doors out in the country in those days.

The fugitives demanded money. There was no cash in the house. They tied my parents in separate bedrooms as hostages, threatening to kill them. Having found a shotgun and an old rifle in the porch, they proceeded to shoot through furniture and walls, terrifying my parents.

The younger accomplice, who was eighteen years old, then went outside.

Allan and his wife lived on the same property with their eighteen-month-old girl. Their second baby was due any day.

When Allan saw the younger man walking in the yard, he went out to investigate. Upon his return to their house, he told his wife that he was very suspicious about the man. Something wasn't right. He decided to go to our parents' house to make sure all was well.

When he walked into their home, he was accosted. The men grabbed him and attempted to tie him to a chair. One aimed the rifle and pulled the trigger at close range, killing my brother instantly. His life ended just before his thirty-third birthday.

The criminals left the guns and fled on the stolen motorcycle. One hour later, they were caught and arrested by the police.

This was an incredible shock to our family and our quiet farming community. Other tragic details of the men's crimes left us reeling with disbelief and pain.

In an extraordinary way, our whole family was cocooned in God's grace. Despite the horror, the Lord's peace brought us indescribable comfort. The Bible says that *"the peace of God, which surpasses all understanding, will guard your hearts and minds through Christ Jesus"* (Philippians 4:7).

As my dad's memory deteriorated, Allan, eleven years my senior, had become a father figure in my life. A gentle, patient person, he had been mature beyond his years. Loving and serving Jesus Christ had been the passion of his life. He'd been cheerful, willing, and faithful in every responsibility. He'd been a leader in the church. As often as possible, he had used his music and beautiful singing voice to bring joy and encouragement to others. He had often sung on gospel radio broadcasts.

Although his body now lay in the casket, *Allan was not there*. He was alive in the presence of God.

Heaven became very real to me. I knew I would see him again. The reality of eternal hope came powerfully alive in the words of Jesus:

> Let not your heart be troubled; you believe in God, believe also in Me. In My Father's house are many mansions; if it were not so, I would have told you. I go to prepare a place for you. And if I go and prepare a place for you, I will come again and receive you to Myself; that where I am, there you may be also. (John 14:1–3)

For me, personally, it was never difficult to forgive the criminals. In God's mercy, I realized that no amount of bitterness or hate in my heart could undo what had been done. Forgiveness kept my heart free to move forward.

When tragedy strikes, it has been said there are two ways to ask the question "Why?" One is with a clenched fist; the other, with the open hand of acceptance.

Although I still have many unanswered questions as to why this heartbreak was permitted, I have made the choice to keep an open hand with trust in God. Someday we will gather together before the Lord in eternity. All the answers will be clear and the questions won't matter anymore.

Our family home of more than forty years had to be sold and my father placed in a nursing home. Within six months, my mother lost her son, her home, and her husband. She also had to stand as a crown witness at the trial of the two young men.

She held firmly to her faith in Christ, knowing that the Lord would never leave or forsake her, as He had promised. She demonstrated amazing resilience which can only be attributed to God's grace and supernatural strength. She bounced back despite the pain and questions.

My sister-in-law also experienced trauma. She gave birth to their second daughter two weeks after my brother's death and had to deal with many legal procedures, as well as moving from the farm where she had lived for less than three years. The shock caused much physical and emotional upheaval. Most difficult of all, she now had the daunting challenge of raising two little girls alone.

With great courage, she took the initiative to visit the prison and speak with her husband's murderers. She told them that because she had received God's forgiveness for her sins by His grace, she could offer forgiveness for what they had done. It would be years before we learned that eventually both of those men came to a place of repentance and surrender to Jesus Christ as their Savior.

Forgiveness is a process, but it always begins with a choice. When we choose to forgive as God has forgiven us, His grace is released to work within us. As we take the first step of obedience and surrender to Christ, He does in us that which we cannot do for ourselves. As someone once said, "When you forgive someone, you set a prisoner free and discover the prisoner was you."

Jesus taught us to pray, *"And forgive us our debts, as we forgive our debtors"* (Matthew 6:12). We are all indebted to God. Christ, the perfect Son of God, suffered and died to provide mercy and forgiveness to all who will trust Him. As we read in 1 Peter 3:18, *"For Christ also suffered once for sins, the just for the unjust, that He might bring us to God..."*

One day I shared this experience with a neighbor, a professed atheist. He exclaimed, "I don't understand why God would permit one good man to die so that two bad men could become good!"

From the mouth of the atheist that day, I have rarely heard the message of the gospel so clearly spoken!

Six

GROWING PAINS

*Character cannot be developed in ease
and quiet. Only through experience
of trial and suffering can the soul be
strengthened, ambition inspired,
and success achieved.*[3]
Helen Keller

For a couple of years after my brother's death, I continued to work with the training center, teaching classes and leading various ministry teams. I was very involved in speaking and music ministry as well as helping with visitation, general pastoral care, and evangelism. These experiences enriched and broadened my understanding of teamwork and service to others.

---

[3] Helen Keller, "Character cannot be developed…" *BrainyQuote*. Date of access: August 8, 2023 (https://www.brainyquote.com/quotes/helen_keller_101340).

On one occasion, I spoke in the United States for a few weeks. I felt rather lonesome being away from the hectic schedule of the training center, and upon my return I told the pastor's wife that I wasn't sure I would be able to continue traveling in ministry. I felt so lonely.

Without a speck of compassion, she folded her arms and looked me up and down. "Well, you know what loneliness is," she stated matter-of-factly. "It's ninety-nine percent self-pity!"

I was speechless! She was right. This revelation thoroughly transformed my attitude and has since proven to be the most helpful, practical counsel.

In the years that followed, opportunities and invitations for ministry continued to arrive. A month-long mission tour was arranged for me in Basel, a city in the German-speaking part of Switzerland. The Lord faithfully met with us during these services. More and more, I learned to adapt to different situations and cultures.

My brother Wesley married Dorothy, a lovely woman from west Texas. They raised their children in Big Spring, where he had a photography studio. The entire family was blessed with tremendous artistic and musical talent. They traveled across Texas and several other states singing country gospel music and ministering. They brought inspiration wherever they went. They eventually toured across Canada as well.

I had the opportunity to speak in several churches in their area while visiting. Despite my youth, the ministry advanced and had wonderful success.

However, all was not well for me. I struggled with a sense of uncertainty, perhaps because of conflicts I had encountered. I felt much inner tension. At times I was overwhelmed with the perception that God was disappointed with me.

One evening, I went to a service with my brother and his family in Big Spring. The speaker presented four points to demonstrate the difference between the conviction of the Holy Spirit and the condemnation of the devil:

- Satan always speaks through the reasonings of the mind. The Holy Spirit always speaks through the conscience.
- The devil always brings despair, death, darkness, fear, and hopelessness. The Lord always brings victory, life, light, love, and hope.
- The enemy always attacks using a vague cloud of accusation. When God speaks, He points precisely to the problem and shows the solution.
- Satan will never offer forgiveness. But the mighty power of the blood of Jesus Christ provides forgiveness and cleansing from every sin and failure.

I left the church that evening a changed person, recognizing that I was being deceived by the devil. I had been falling for his lies, which told me that I was a failure and beyond hope.

My heart was lifted to a new level of faith and understanding of God's amazing grace. In Christ, we are more than conquerors.

> There is therefore now no condemnation to those who are in Christ Jesus, who do not walk according to the flesh, but according to the Spirit. For the law of the Spirit of life in Christ Jesus has made me free from the law of sin and death. (Romans 8:1–2)

From Texas, I went to Mexico with a missionary couple. I was struck by the contrast between affluent America and the poverty south of the Rio Grande.

Eating beans and hot peppers in a handmade tortilla was a new experience—especially the hot peppers! Because there was no refrigeration, the only safe option for me to drink was lukewarm cola. When the warm cola, beans, and peppers got together, I felt like a helium balloon. I was sure I could float clear to the North Pole!

As we ate in an adobe hut one day, I kept a wary eye on the chickens perched on the wire above my head. I didn't want any unexpected additions to my tortilla! Another distraction was the mother pig and three little ones under the table...

I was deeply impressed by the people's sincerity of faith and commitment. We gathered for outdoor services in the warm evenings. Under the trees, we sang and praised the Lord. I preached and prayed for these beautiful folk. The Lord was present, doing His amazing work in their souls.

In 1977, I was ordained into the ministry and had the opportunity to travel to a ministers conference in London, Ontario. Pastor Harry Wuerch was one of the highly respected pastors at the conference, and he invited me to speak at his church. As a result, other pastors in the area opened the doors of their assemblies for me to share Christ.

The next year, I made an extended ministry tour through several cities and towns in Ontario. In every place, the Lord touched hearts and His Word brought encouragement.

I had just arrived in London, Ontario when word came that my father had passed away. I found myself taking a flight back to Saskatchewan for his funeral. The assurance of God's care surrounded our family. Hope in Christ gave us comfort and assurance once more.

In August 1979, I prepared an itinerary which would include several months of ministry in eastern Canada and the United States. I didn't realize it then, but this would be the beginning of a trip which would never really end.

Seven

EXPANDING VISION

*Abraham wasn't perfect. He failed, made
mistakes. But, he would go back, get right
with God, and then just keep moving
forward. He didn't quit when things
got hard. He just kept on going. And
everywhere he went, God was there.
God was with him.*[4]
Anne Graham Lotz

Plans were put in place for me to go on an extensive
mission trip using the contacts of several missionaries
I had met. The tour would take me through the Caribbean

[4] Anne Graham Lotz, "Abraham wasn't perfect…" *BrainyQuote.* Date of
access: August 8, 2023 (https://www.brainyquote.com/quotes/anne_graham_
lotz_571042).

and South America for several months in the winter and spring of 1980.

Leaving my car at my brother's home in Texas, I flew to Jamaica where I was invited to speak in numerous churches over a one-month period. The pastor there took me under his wing, giving opportunities to minister in various parts of the island.

The hospitality and kindness of the people deeply touched my heart. It was also a time filled with new experiences. In that one month, I ate more than forty foods I had never seen before. Most of the tropical foods were delicious… others, not so much!

The youth were especially responsive. Every evening they lined the altars in prayer. Sometimes I joined them as they walked together in groups on their way home after the service. They sang all the way home in the warm, moonlit nights.

From Jamaica, I went on to Haiti for one week. It was a jolt to observe such abject poverty. It was the first time I witnessed people searching for food in garbage cans. One of the churches where I spoke was literally a shack up in the mountains, but the believers were enthusiastic and earnest.

As my departing airplane gained speed on takeoff from Port-au-Prince, suddenly I heard several loud explosions. Flames shot out of the motor on the left side of the aircraft. The plane jerked violently before coming to an abrupt stop.

We sat on the runway for several hours as repair crews worked through the night. I'm not sure what the problem was, but I did quite a bit of praying and preparing for heaven! Later I heard that the cause may have been debris, or perhaps birds that had been sucked into the motor.

One thing was certain: I was very glad to land safely in Bogotá, Colombia. There, Pastor Sixto Lopez and his wife had prepared for me to speak at a series of special services. He also had a very effective radio ministry.

One evening, several people from high in the Andes attended the service, and a group of them came up to me after the meeting. Through the interpreter, they told me that they had understood me while I had been praying in other tongues. I was astounded! The Holy Spirit had seen their hungry hearts and confirmed the gospel of Jesus Christ.

From Colombia, I went to Peru. After preaching in Lima, I traveled many hours north by bus with Nina, a young evangelist from the local church. She served as my translator and proved to be a great travel companion. We ministered in the city of Chiclayo near the Ecuadorian border where two young Peruvian women were starting a church. The group was small but passionate for the Lord.

The room where these women lived was near a marketplace. The unusual smells wafting from below were almost overpowering. The women had purchased three chickens before our arrival. Each one had a leg tied to the table leg. The chickens clucked and scratched as they ate the crumbs on the floor. Every day or so, I would notice there was one chicken less. Rice and chicken made a tasty meal!

After three weeks in Peru, I traveled to Brazil. Several months before, I had written to a missionary family in Brazil and informed them of my flight number and arrival time. When I landed in São Paulo, however, no one was there to meet me. I waited and wondered… and then I worried, becoming very concerned. The airport was about to close for the night and I was told I had to leave.

Looking out of the window of my hotel at the lights of the vast city, I felt very alone. What was I to do? In my naivety, I hadn't thought to bring the telephone number or street address for this missionary family. All I had was a post office box address.

Gazing at the millions of city lights, the morbid thought passed through my mind that I could just disappear here. People would say, "Yes, she went to Brazil and was never seen again…"

This gave me great incentive to pray! I called out to the Lord for His help and direction. And then a plan formed in my mind.

Early the next morning, I sat on my suitcase in the hotel lobby and asked every person who came in, "Can you speak English?"

Finally, a very handsome young man arrived. He replied, "Yes, I speak a little English."

When I explained my dilemma, he looked at the post office address I had and shook his head. "That town is thirty kilometers away. There is no bus. Taxi would be mucho-mucho."

Then, with a flash of inspiration, he said, "Me take you!"

The thought passed through my mind that if I was going to disappear, it may as well be with this very handsome young man!

Being from the backcountry of western Canada, I had limited knowledge of the intricacies of such a vast city. I thought that I would visit this post office in the missionaries' town and hope that the workers there could provide me with the family's street address. If not, then perhaps someone from the family would show up soon to check their mail!

It was a crazy plan—but it worked and we soon arrived at the missionaries' home. What a relief!

It turned out that the missionaries, Mr. and Mrs. Lambeth, had never received my letter. Furthermore, they were preparing to leave on a three-day outing. If I had arrived even fifteen minutes later, they would have already been gone.

As part of their mission, they had founded several small outposts, and we had a service at one almost every evening for the next six weeks. The buildings were packed.

It was hot and dusty as people sat, stood, or peered in through the open windows. On the weekends hundreds of folks would gather in the central church, which held nearly two thousand people.

The Lord was powerfully present, bringing salvation, healing, and baptizing many in the Holy Spirit. It was an amazing mission tour filled with important experiences and learning opportunities. Time and again I saw the divine intervention of the Lord.

And despite my inexperience and naivety, He brought me safely back to Canada.

Eight

EUROPEAN ADVENTURES

Delight yourself also in the Lord, and He
shall give you the desires of your heart.
Commit your way to the Lord, trust also in
Him, and He shall bring it to pass.
Psalm 37:4–5

Upon my return, I invited a good friend, Glenda Atcheson, to travel with me on my next trip. She was contagiously cheerful as well as a gifted musician. Although already preparing to work in Mexico, she agreed to accompany me on a ministry tour through eastern Canada and then Europe in the fall of 1980.

Another good friend, Karl Kienle, who had attended the same Bible training center as me, had preached in several countries of Europe the previous year. He had spoken to various pastors about inviting me to speak in their churches, but they were somewhat reticent to receive me. Women ministers were virtually unknown in Europe at that time—and one particular pastor was adamantly opposed to the idea, although he was finally persuaded to let me preach in his church for a week.

With these contacts from Karl and others, I was able to make an itinerary through England, Belgium, and Switzerland. Glenda's testimony and music proved to be a huge blessing and inspiration. I was grateful for her sense of humor and lively companionship. We weren't accustomed to the high humidity, continuous rain, and lack of central heating in England, though, and felt very nearly frozen almost the entire time we were there. But the Lord certainly was present during the services.

After one service, the people gathered about us to pray for God's blessing on our future journeys. The pastor delivered a clear message from the Lord telling us not to be afraid, that God would go before us and make a way where there seemed no way.

Then he added, "Don't be concerned for finances, as you will know no lack." That proved to be a true prophetic word.

People have often asked me, "Where do you get your money?" I can truthfully say that God has been faithful. Most of the finances for this ministry have come through church offerings as well as individuals who have been touched by the Lord as a result of the services.

I live simply and am quite cheap to keep! I have never asked for money. However, I have a deep awareness that any resources I receive belong to God. Realizing that I will give an account to the Lord for every dollar reminds me to remain conscientious and thrifty.

Glenda and I finally began to thaw out when we arrived in Belgium. One of the places where we ministered was in the city of Flenu. The visionary pastor, Guy Guilbert, was a gifted organizer with a heart to reach as many people as possible with the gospel. The building was filled to capacity every evening. Dozens gave their hearts to Christie. We heard amazing testimonies of healing from heart conditions, cancer, and back problems, as well as various other diseases.

The gift of the word of knowledge[5] concerning health conditions operated very strongly. One night, a young lady came up for prayer. She had received radiation treatments for cancer and the doctors had told her it would be impossible for her to ever have a child. By inspiration of the Holy Spirit, I told her that she would have a son, which came to pass nine months later. God miraculously overruled what the doctors had told her.

We arrived in Switzerland at the end of November. The Lord gave us great favor during our services in the church in Lausanne with Pastor Henri Heytons. I was a bit of a novelty, a young woman from an unpronounceable

---

[5] The gifts of the Holy Spirit are listed in 1 Corinthians 12:7–11.

province in Canada, singing country gospel music—and preaching. They had never seen anything quite like it! Dozens of people responded for salvation and others received healing in answer to prayer.

When we arrived in the canton of Valais, we were met by a friendly, energetic man named Willy Droz. It was a relief that he could speak fluent English, as his wife Brenda was from England. They graciously welcomed us.

After we had eaten supper the first evening, we spent some time getting acquainted. Then Pastor Droz dropped a bombshell: "Women in ministry are not at all accepted in the French-speaking parts of Europe. But we have arranged some small meetings for this week. We'll see how it goes."

I was shocked and deeply dismayed! I desperately needed the Lord to stand by me. Only He could supply wisdom, courage, and strength in the face of this skepticism. Glenda and I earnestly prayed for God's favor and spiritual breakthrough.

The church in the area of Martigny, Switzerland was a pioneer work in a spiritually dark corner of the nation. Pastor Droz had courageously begun the assembly a couple of years before with a handful of believers.

That week of outreach services made an impact on the region. People came to Jesus. Some folks were healed and others received the baptism of the Holy Spirit. Night after night, the meeting room was jampacked with people.

When it was time to return to Canada, Pastor Droz prepared to take us to the airport. He asked if I would consider returning. I was astonished and thrilled! I told him that I would be pleased to return if he would be willing to make the arrangements. I didn't speak the language or have many contacts, so I would have to depend on his assistance. He told me he would be glad to look after every detail.

"How much time should I leave open?" I asked.

"Five months."

I was astonished all over again! It was only later that I learned he was the pastor who had been the most opposed to my coming.

I discovered that Pastor Droz had a tremendous gift to organize and facilitate. I hadn't fully realized how many contacts he had across Switzerland, France, Belgium, and other countries as well.

True to his word, he began preparations for my next visit to Europe. The Lord had led me to connect with the person who would eventually, directly and indirectly, be the link to open all of western Europe to this ministry.

Nine

ROMANTIC DISTRACTION

*Therefore we also, since we are surrounded
by so great a cloud of witnesses, let us lay
aside every weight, and the sin which so
easily ensnares us, and let us run with
endurance the race that is set before us,
looking unto Jesus, the author
and finisher of our faith…*
Hebrews 12:1–2

For several months, I communicated with a young man, the assistant pastor of a Canadian church I had visited. It was so pleasant to have his attention. His letters were filled with kind words and various sweet nothings.

Over the years, a number of young men had expressed romantic interest in me. In fact, in every place I visited I kept my eyes open for eligible bachelors. I did not travel about with my eyes closed!

However, no one I met measured up to my expectations. I wholeheartedly agreed when someone aptly quipped, "I never met anyone going the same direction at the same speed!"

But this young man was very persistent. His letters and phone calls were flattering to a lonesome heart.

After returning from our ministry tour in Europe, Glenda left to further her Bible school and language studies in preparation for missionary outreach in Mexico. I had begun a ministry tour across Alberta and British Columbia where amazing and exciting opportunities had opened for me to share the gospel.

In Golden, British Columbia, each evening I met with a group of recently converted young people. Many had come from the hippie movement and now passionately pursued Christ. We had a tremendous time studying the Word of God together for several days.

When it came time to leave, I was very short of cash. Determined not to mention my need to anyone, I earnestly prayed for provision. The next stop was several hundred kilometers away.

As I started to drive off, one young man came running toward my car, his long, shaggy hair billowing like a bush. I stopped as he reached for the door handle.

Pushing his bushy hair in through the window, he whispered, "I'm sure you don't need it, but I felt I should give you this money."

He pressed a one-hundred-dollar bill into my hand!

Hot tears flooded my eyes as I drove away. The young man wouldn't have had any way of knowing how timely his gift was. My heart was filled with praise to God for His great faithfulness.

I felt impressed to rent a public hall in the village of Faust in northwestern Alberta. It was a daring venture, as I knew practically no one in the area. On the first night, about twenty folks showed up. For the second evening, about fifty. For the third, the place was packed with standing room only. Several people received Christ and we heard some glorious testimonies of healing.

Throughout this journey, the near-daily telephone calls and frequent letters from this amorous and perseverant gentleman followed me. In the deepest part of my heart, I knew this relationship was not God's will for me. In fact, a woman of God had warned me not to continue with this romance some months before. However, loud excuses had competed with God's voice: "It's hard to be alone. You could do much more together. He's a kind man. He loves the Lord. He's in ministry."

For many reasons it all seemed so right. But I had no peace.

Although I knew this relationship was not to be, I continued to enjoy the attention and the warm, fuzzy sentiments. I found myself descending into a place of confusion and frustration. My will was fighting against God's will.

Ever since that experience, I've had an answer for anyone who tells me they're confused and frustrated about a situation: "Submit to God. Stop fighting against what you know is the Lord's will. It's impossible to experience the peace of God while rebelling against Him. A basic cause of stress is living against one's values."

After one of those long telephone calls, I felt especially troubled. At that time, I was staying with Lorne and Mavis, a couple who had a keen prophetic gifting. They knew nothing of the situation. Overwhelmed and discouraged, I asked them to pray for me.

What she stated next changed my destiny.

"Yes, the problem is about a young man," said Mavis. "You are permitting him to pursue you, even though you know marriage to him is not God's will for you. I see a vision of a road which dead-ends at a crossroads like a giant T. On one side of the T is a garbage dump; on the other is a graveyard. He is standing at the crossroads. If you continue walking the way you are going, you will marry him. When you do, the anointing of God will lift off your life. Your ministry will end like a heap of trash and you will die a young and unhappy woman."

God had nailed me! I knew this woman spoke the truth. The Lord had my full attention—and finally I heard His message.

That very night, I wrote a letter ending the relationship. Almost immediately I was filled with peace. The confusion was gone. A profound assurance of God's presence and favor flooded my heart.

Life is comprised of moments in which our decisions determine our destiny. Choosing to trust and obey God produces life and hope. And with the passing of years, God's love has been sufficient for me; His grace, abundant. His faithfulness has provided everything I've ever needed, even beyond my dreams.

I can truly agree with the adage that says, "I would rather be single than wish I was!" Besides, at this point it seems that all the good men are either married or buried!

Anita Pearce
at age two.

Anita in her mother's
flower garden
at age five.

*Anita's Grade Two
school picture
at age eight.*

*Anita as a young
evangelist in 1977.*

*Anita's mother
and father in
about 1970.*

*Anita's mom,
age ninety-five,
in 2008.*

*Anita's oldest
brother Wesley
and his piano
accordion in 2008.*

*Anita's brother Allan beside his
farm tractor in 1974.*

*Anita's older sister
Velma at the piano.*

Pastor Karl and Darlene Kienle in New Life Community Church, Kuroki, Saskatchewan in 2010.

Pastor and Mrs. Droz as we returned on the train from ministry in Ukraine in 2002.

Christelle Colant translating for Anita in Chalon-sur-Saone, France in 2011.

Laetitia Marq and Anita traveling together in Alberta, Canada in 2009.

Anita preaching at Selwyn Outreach Center near Peterborough, Ontario in 2010.

Anita with folks who have responded for prayer.

The staff of Inspiration Ministries sharing a meal with Anita in 2014.

—Karen Bashforth, Leanne Simpson, and Darlene Kienle—

Ten

HOME BASE

*Brethren, I do not count myself to have
apprehended; but one thing I do, forgetting
those things which are behind and reaching
forward to those things which are ahead,
I press toward the goal for the prize of the
upward call of God in Christ Jesus.*
Philippians 3:13–14

Until early 1981, after my trips I had always returned to the training center where I had a dormitory room. I was grateful for this provision but realized it would soon be necessary to find a place where I could set up my own home and office.

I searched for a suitable location where I could establish a home base. I needed three things:

- a local church where I could get involved when I was home, with a pastor who would understand my vision.
- someone trustworthy who could handle the office administration.
- a relatively inexpensive location, as I had a very limited amount of money.

Karl Kienle had been a family friend for many years. His wife Darlene and I had become close friends during Bible school. Once they were married, they were led to plant a church in the village of Margo, Saskatchewan, population about two hundred.

Therefore, when I chose to move to Margo, Karl became my pastor and Darlene my secretary. I was able to purchase a sixty-five-square-meter mobile home. At that time, there was no place more economical to live than a small village in Saskatchewan. At last, I had a nest of my own.

Darlene has been a great blessing to me. For more than forty years, we have worked hand in glove. Talented and highly intelligent, her office administration abilities and computer skills have been invaluable. I tell folks that although I do all the talking, she is the brainpower!

She has kept the office running effectively and efficiently. As a very good friend, she has often been my confidante when I've been confronted with dilemmas. On occasion she has dared to offer clarity and correction.

As for Pastor Karl, he has been a solid, steady man of courage and tenacity—a tremendous example of faithfulness and commitment to Christ.

The Lord truly was faithful to provide the perfect place for me to call home. With a home base established, I packed up and continued my travels.

Across the west of Canada I journeyed. Many doors opened to minister, and with each opportunity people came to Jesus and were healed. Everywhere I went, folks seemed to receive encouragement.

One night after a service, I joined the family with whom I was staying to watch the evening news. Included in the broadcast was the story of six members of a family who had been murdered. Their bodies had been located in a burned-out motor home driven off a cliff in the mountains. What a gruesome story to watch before going to bed!

That night, I was attacked by overwhelming fear. My lively imagination conjured up all kinds of horrors. What if I had a car accident? What if I got sick? What if I ran out of money?

With very little sleep, I left the next morning for the Yukon. At that time, the Alaska Highway was about two thousand kilometers of gravel road through desolate wilderness.

The voice of fear faded during the day, but at night my imagination seemed to go crazy. Peace would come only after much prayer and consistently speaking promises from the Word of God. This battle continued for many months.

After several weeks of ministry in the Yukon, I visited cities throughout the northwest before returning home. That autumn, a new itinerary was prepared which would bring me to communities in Alberta and British Columbia.

Although the Lord worked powerfully in the services, the unreasonable fear returned almost every night. While staying in the home of a friend, she asked me if I'd ever had a problem with fear. I told her about my struggle. As we prayed together, I felt a great release. The anguish was gone.

Almost that same day, I read the following comment on an inspirational calendar: "God does not give us grace for our imagination. He gives us grace for our experience." I have since realized that God has given us the right to decide what we meditate on. We can refuse to fill our minds with unprofitable and destructive thoughts.

It has been said that ninety-eight percent of our worries will never come true. The two percent that do transpire never happen the way we planned! Another axiom states, "Worrying is using your imagination to create things you don't want." I've suffered various anxieties and fears throughout the years, but the mind-destroying torment of that season has never returned.

As I traveled from place to place, I established a certain rhythm of Bible study, prayer, and sermon preparation—a rhythm which I maintain to this day. Usually my mornings are spent seeking the Lord for the message He would have me share each evening. Occasionally, this has to be done on the fly as I travel from place to place. Sometimes inspiration has been very hard to find. Prayer, perseverance, and perspiration are the formula!

I never did have much time or interest in sports, but I greatly enjoy walking. It provides physical exercise, mental stimulation, as well as an opportunity for prayer and meditation. As often as possible, it has become my habit to find time and relatively safe places where I can enjoy an hour or so of walking while I pray.

This discipline has been very beneficial for body, soul, and spirit.

Eleven

LONGER JOURNEYS

Now to Him who is able to do exceedingly
abundantly above all that we ask
or think, according to the power
that works in us...
Ephesians 3:20

Pastor Droz did a masterful job of preparing the itinerary for my next five-month ministry tour of Europe in the spring of 1982. A friend, Nancy Thorstad, joined me on this trip. As well as being a talented pianist, she had a basic understanding of French. What a blessing it was to have her assistance!

The schedule was very hectic. In the area of Lyon, France, Pastor Claude Stalin had arranged nearly thirty services in two weeks. By the end of our time there, I was exhausted.

Shortly after arriving at the next location in northern France, however, I became quite ill. The local church leader, who just happened to be a medical doctor, diagnosed me with a gallbladder attack brought on by intense fatigue. He gave me an injection that improved my condition. I felt very weak and shaky, but by clinging tightly to the pulpit I was able to preach that same afternoon.

I experienced the grace that God gave Apostle Paul: *"For when I am weak, then I am strong"* (2 Corinthians 12:10). Dozens of people in that place responded by giving their lives to Christ.

During a service in Belgium, I received a clear word of knowledge about a man present who was plotting a murder. No one moved.

Suddenly, a middle-aged man jumped to his feet and literally ran to the altar sobbing. Together with the pastor and others in leadership, we were able to pray with him. With deep repentance, he surrendered his life and the situation into the Lord's hands.

Opportunities came again for ministry in eastern Canada during the summer of 1983. I loaded my little car with everything I would need for several months. As I drove east, I was distracted by the wheat fields. The crop was beautiful and clean on one side of the highway, while on the other side the crop was sparse and full of weeds. There had to be a spiritual lesson in it.

Engrossed in surveying the fields, I didn't notice the signs warning of construction ahead—and when my attention returned to the highway, three cars were stopped less than forty meters in front of me. With screeching brakes and burning rubber, I plowed into the back of the nearest car, which in turn rammed the next vehicle.

When the dust cleared, miraculously there were no serious injuries. I was stiff for several weeks and had minor cuts and bruises from the seatbelt. My car was no longer drivable or fixable.

The police took me to a hotel. My sister and brother-in-law drove five hours to pick me up. They took me car shopping and helped me get on my way again.

The story could have turned out very differently. In mercy, the Lord had surrounded me with His protection, provision, and presence.

That journey took me across Ontario, Quebec, and into the Maritimes, with many encouraging results.

Pastor Droz then invited me to return to Europe. He arranged a full nine months of ministry across western Europe in 1984. Most of the ministry was in Switzerland, France, and Belgium, with brief excursions to other countries, including England, Scotland, Sweden, and Spain.

With the help of cassettes and books, I learned basic French. Reading my Bible in French and being forced to communicate with my limited vocabulary, I slowly began to understand the language. I was very grateful for the excellent interpreters who worked with me.

The cuisine in south and central France is delicious and particularly celebrated for its elegant presentation. I learned very quickly not to fill my plate with the first course, since there would be six or seven more! And one should never think a meal will be over in a few minutes, as in Canada. Often I would be seated about noon and not get up from the meal until the late afternoon. The French way is to debate and discuss deep matters around the table.

This was a trial for a country bumpkin like me. I fumbled about in my limited knowledge of the language while trying to sort out the three or four forks and different knives! I often pretended that I knew what I was doing.

I had learned a catchy little chorus, written by Jerry Goff, which a friend helped me to translate to French, called "I Am Blessed." It became a sort of theme song when I traveled in the French-speaking countries, as well as other places.

In Europe, our services usually ran from Tuesday to Sunday, with Mondays being spent traveling from place to place, typically by train. The schedule was rigorous, averaging about eight services per week.

We often held special after-meetings on Friday and Saturday nights. An evening's first service would have an evangelistic emphasis, giving people the opportunity to respond to the gospel for salvation. In the after-meeting, I would teach and then pray for folks to receive the baptism of the Holy Spirit. The second service would usually start about fifteen minutes after the first finished.

During one after-meeting in Geneva, nearly one hundred people stayed for the infilling and renewal of the Holy Spirit. My translator interpreted from English to French, although she was an Italian firecracker! Together we watched the mighty power of the Holy Spirit fall upon people. I was bouncing around, praying aloud in other tongues, and laying hands on those who were intently seeking the Lord. Nearly everyone received the baptism of the Holy Spirit.

A little lady came to speak to us after the service. She excitedly told me through the interpreter, "When you laid hands on me, you not only spoke Sicilian, you spoke the dialect of my village in Sicily!"

I was astounded. "What did I say?"

"The instant you put your hands on my head, you clearly spoke in my dialect, saying, 'At this moment you are released in the Holy Spirit.' A geyser erupted within me and I began to speak with other tongues!"

The Lord uses amazing signs and wonders to confirm His love and power!

I haven't kept track of numbers. Only God knows how many lives have been touched. Dozens, if not hundreds, of people have given their lives to Christ and received the baptism of the Holy Spirit. I have seen and heard so many outstanding testimonies of healing as well.

Sometimes I wonder why everyone isn't instantly healed when they receive prayer in the name of Jesus. I don't know the answer. It's a question which only eternity will resolve. I certainly do not claim any particular gift of healing, although I stand upon the promise of Mark 16:17–18:

> And these signs will follow those who believe: in My name they will cast out demons; they will speak with new tongues; they will take up serpents; and if they drink anything deadly, it will by no means hurt them; they will lay hands on the sick, and they will recover.

Therefore, I continue to pray and trust the Lord to do His work. I will rejoice in His manifested power and leave the mysteries in His hands.

One evening in Cambrai, France, a young woman who had been in a skiing accident came up for prayer. A twenty-centimeter steel plate had been used to repair the severe damage to her knee. She had been told she would never bend her leg again.

When we prayed that evening, nothing happened.

But the next day, as she sat at her office desk, one of her coworkers exclaimed, "What has happened to your leg?"

When she looked down, the young woman realized that she was sitting with her knee bent normally.

"I've been healed!" she shrieked.

At the next evening's service, she walked and ran about the church demonstrating to us all what God had done.

I later received word that when she returned to her doctor, he examined her and was absolutely amazed—and puzzled.

"But what has happened to my piece of steel?" he said. "The x-rays can find no trace of it."

The knee was like brand new. Glory to God!

On another occasion, as I sang the song "He Touched Me," I saw a man come into the service and sit at the back. Even at that distance, I was aware that he wept through most of the message.

When I invited folks to come to Christ, he jumped from his chair and quickly moved toward the front, weeping all the way.

Later I heard his story. He was in despair because his wife had left him, his job was in jeopardy, and alcohol was controlling his life. He had parked his car on the street near the church and placed a pistol under the front seat.

Planning to end it all, he walked past the church on his way to a nearby shop to buy bullets. But as he heard the hope-filled words of the song, he was drawn inside. There, he heard that Jesus Christ could set him free and change his life.

That night, he was transformed by the power of God. He was saved and delivered. The promise of God's Word became real in his life: *"Therefore, if anyone is in Christ, he is a new creation; old things have passed away; behold, all things have become new"* (2 Corinthians 5:17).

Twelve

GREATER ASSIGNMENTS

When you get into a tight place and
everything goes against you, till it seems as
though you could not hang on a minute
longer, never give up then, for that is just
the place and time that the tide will turn.[6]
Harriet Beecher Stowe

Year by year, the ministry tours lengthened as I traveled across Canada and other countries.

Message preparation has always been a time-consuming and challenging work for me. My style has been to prepare Biblical, practical, and easily understood messages, emphasizing certain points for clarity. Often I've

---

[6] Harriet Beecher Stowe, "Never Give Up Quotes to Keep You Going," *Keepinspiring.me*. March 20, 23023 (https://www.keepinspiring.me/never-give-up-quotes).

followed the same outlines as I go from place to place, believing those messages can bring blessing to different congregations.

I kept the outlines in notebooks and stored them in a large handbag. Shortly after arriving in St. John, New Brunswick in the spring of 1986, I left my car parked on the street in front of a church while I went for supper with the pastor and his wife. I took my wallet with me but foolishly left my handbag in the car—on the front seat, no less.

When I returned, the car window had been smashed and the handbag was gone. I was horrified!

I knew the handbag held no money, a fact the thieves could not have known! It must have been rather disappointing for them to find nothing but a Bible and some sermon notes. Someone later suggested to me that they may have gotten saved and become preachers, using my sermons!

Thankfully I had kept many scraps of paper with original outlines. It was a lot of work, but I was able to recover and retype much of the lost material.

In the autumn of 1986, I had the opportunity to minister at churches in Uganda and Kenya. While in East Africa, I also taught briefly in a Bible school. This was my only visit to Africa, but other missionaries have done exceptional work in these nations.

The following year, I returned to Europe for another five-month tour. For several years, my schedule had been quite hectic, averaging about three hundred services per year, in many different climates and conditions. My voice began to be raspy and hoarse constantly, and it was difficult to sing and speak. The doctor told me that nodules were forming on my vocal cords. The solution would involve either complete voice rest or surgery.

When I returned from Europe, I was forced to take a three-month sabbatical, from June to September 1987, for voice rest. That meant no singing, no speaking, and no whispering. I was also supposed to learn to speak and sing without strain.

Speechless? What a challenge! However, at the end of three months the doctor told me that the nodules were gone. I was intensely grateful for God's grace in helping me to keep quiet. I'm sure others were appreciative as well!

Later that year, I formed Inspiration Ministries, a government-recognized charitable organization. The oversight of the board of directors continues to provide financial accountability and credibility. I am so thankful for the people of integrity and wisdom who have served on the board with me.

My ministry tours then expanded to Scandinavia. One pastor knew another, who was related to another, who then opened a door someplace else. Opportunities spread from Finland to Sweden and Denmark, even to remote places like Iceland and Greenland.

The services in Borga, Finland started on a Wednesday evening. A man of about sixty sat on the seat directly in front of me as I stood behind the pulpit. He was very attentive, and when I invited people to come for prayer he immediately jumped to his feet and came forward.

Every evening for the rest of the week, this man took his place in exactly the same spot. Each time, he reacted quickly when the call came to receive prayer.

On Sunday night, I noticed a woman sitting beside him. At the end of the message, he took her hand and brought her up for prayer as well. It was his estranged wife. I could tell that the Lord had met him in a special way during the services.

When I returned several years later, the same man met me—only now he was wearing a three-piece suit and looking the part of a dapper gentleman.

He told me his story. He had been one of the wealthiest men in the city before alcohol took control of his life. He lost his money, his job, his wife, and his children.

While searching for food in trash bins, someone had shown compassion and brought him to a rehabilitation center. Later, upon hearing the gospel at my services, the Holy Spirit powerfully touched his life.

His family was restored and he was now working in the rehab center, helping others come to Christ.

The Lord did His great work, and people came to Jesus wherever I went. Some were healed and others received the baptism of the Holy Spirit.

On a cold Friday evening in October in Copenhagen, Denmark, a skimpily dressed young woman came into the service, probably to get warm. Christina was a prostitute. Her arms were covered with needle tracks. She listened to the message, wide-eyed, as she heard the gospel of forgiveness and salvation. She quickly responded and gave her life to Christ.

The next evening, she was waiting at the door with other friends from the streets. They also came forward for prayer.

On Sunday evening, she came again, this time with a great number of street people. There were drug addicts, prostitutes, and alcoholics—all her friends from the dark haunts of the city. They filled the auditorium and crammed the balcony.

When the opportunity came to surrender to Christ, dozens of these precious souls rushed forward to meet with God. It was an incredible experience to see the power of God transform so many hearts.

Standing on the platform beside me was a large wooden cross. One young man came right up beside me and fell to his knees in front of the cross. With tears pouring down his cheeks, he carefully caressed and clung to that cross.

When I returned to the same church three years later, Christina was one of the first to meet me. She had spent one year in a drug rehabilitation center, then attended Bible school for one year. Now for one year she had been married to a fine young man. The power of God had accomplished a mighty work of grace in her life.

On November 9, 1989, I watched the evening news together with friends in Denmark. The Berlin wall had been breached. Thousands of people had streamed across the barrier. The former Soviet Union was disintegrating in front of our eyes!

About a year later, I stood beside the remnants of that very wall. Some of the youth from the church where I was preaching in Berlin joined me with hammers. We broke pieces of the cement to take home as souvenirs. The impregnable kingdoms of men rapidly collapse into dust before Almighty God.

Gudrun Forss, a Swedish missionary who worked with an outreach organization in Brussels, became a good friend of mine. For several years while she was there, she offered to let me use her apartment as a base while I was in Europe. The difficulties of jetlag made it easier to stay in Europe for several months at a time.

Gudrun's home was a good central location from which I could easily travel to other countries. What a tremendous blessing! She also took time to teach me the basics of technology, helping me adapt to using computers.

Thirteen

New Horizons

*Fear not, for I am with you; be not
dismayed, for I am your God. I will
strengthen you, yes, I will help you, I will
uphold you with My righteous right hand.*
Isaiah 41:10

Cassette tapes became very popular. I discovered rather quickly that recording and duplicating sermons was an effective way of spreading the gospel.

Once we purchased the equipment, it was easy to mass-produce and distribute these compact messengers of hope. Hundreds of cassettes were sold and circulated as I traveled about preaching in various assemblies.

I also made a couple of amateur attempts to produce a music recording.

However, I met Dr. Harry Yates when he came to speak at our church in Saskatchewan. His wife, Joanne Cash Yates, is the sister of the famous entertainer, Johnny Cash.

Harry and Joanne, who had been producing country gospel music in Nashville for many years, invited me to go there to make a recording in 1988. What a tremendous privilege it was to work with the best in the business! God supernaturally orchestrated the details.

This was the first of seven country gospel recordings I eventually made in Nashville. All were produced by Dr. Harry Yates and most were recorded at Gene Breeden Studios. Harry and Joanne were very kind and hospitable.

While in Nashville, I was given opportunities to minister in various churches.

After the regular Grand Ole Opry Show, Jimmie Snow would host the late-night Grand Ole Gospel Time. Well-known music stars sang before he preached. Harry arranged for me to sing as well. Standing on that world-famous platform, blinded by the dazzling lights, I had a super bad case of stage fright, but I sang with all my heart for the glory of God!

Each time I made a recording, I was also honored to share at Cowboy Church. This was a fantastic outreach in downtown Nashville. The meetings were held in a well-known auditorium where many were drawn to hear Joanne Cash Yates sing. Other gospel musicians shared as well, after which Harry would preach a powerful message of hope in Christ. It was an amazing vision to reach many with the gospel.

In Nashville, I was exposed to the rich and famous. Despite being surrounded by opulence and temptations for fame and fortune, I found many true hearts who served Christ with humility and commitment.

With the sale of music and ministry materials, it became possible to sponsor other missions. What a privilege it has been to share the provision of the Lord, especially with dozens of needy children.

New adventures were coming! Together with a middle-aged widow, Judy Brown, we planned a mission trip to four Asian countries in May and June of 1992. Judy had been to these nations and had some understanding of the cultures we would encounter. I was so grateful for her help and steady head.

Judy had a beautiful testimony of the Lord's faithfulness to watch over her and direct her following her husband's tragic death in a car accident. Through it all, she had found amazing opportunities to minister, particularly to hurting and broken women. She had worked closely with Women's Aglow as well as the leadership of other outreaches.

We conducted several services in the Philippines before arriving for a couple of weeks of meetings in Taiwan. Dave and Beverly Bedwell had done a tremendous work in the city of Tainan. Besides building a local church, they had established an amazing program to help single mothers.

The Bedwells arranged for us to minister at a retreat at a prayer mountain center. We also had several opportunities to share the gospel with a wonderful church in the city of Taipei.

Arrangements had been made for us to stay in an apartment owned by the church. One morning when I was preparing to get into the shower, an unexpected visitor showed up in the bathtub: a black creature about twenty centimeters long with an abundance of eight-centimeter legs—about one hundred, I would guess!

I called Judy to come and see. Happily, it couldn't seem to climb up the walls of the tub. While taking a video of it, she coolly stated, "I think I'll pass on a shower this morning."

That sounded like a good plan!

One service was also arranged in Hong Kong, which was still under British rule at the time. While there, we linked up with a unique mission involved in smuggling Bibles into mainland China.

That was an escapade to remember. We were caught! The Bibles were confiscated. However, because we were Canadians we were free to enter the country. We stayed one night in China and did a little sightseeing.

Judy immediately noticed that the lamp in our hotel room had been bugged. Calmly, she turned on the television and made signs telling me to zip my lips! We hoped the noise of the TV would drown out any slip of the tongue. I was as nervous as a cat on a hot stove.

From there, we went on to Japan. What an honor it was to share with the seasoned missionaries working in this beautiful country. The spiritual need of Japan particularly moved me. Less than one percent of the population had ever heard the gospel and idolatry was prevalent. However, there was an intense desire to follow Christ in the small groups to whom we ministered.

One Sunday morning in Yokohama, I ministered about the faithfulness of the God who sees, who knows, and who cares for His people. The pastor burst into tears, something which was unusual in this emotionally conservative culture. We discovered that he had been experiencing tremendous pressures. The message had been a prophetic word of hope to his heart. He was greatly encouraged in the Lord.

We traveled extensively by train and subway while in Japan. The multitudes of people riding up the escalators to exit the subway stations reminded me of an upside-down waterfall. Millions of precious souls poured out onto the streets.

One morning, we crossed Tokyo on the train during rush hour. White-gloved workers assisted people to board by pushing and packing them tightly into the train so the doors could slide shut. We were crammed in like sardines in a can.

We took a side trip to Hiroshima, where displays at the museum portray the tragedy of the nuclear devastation of 1945. The tremendous heat of the initial blast had literally vaporized more than thirty thousand soldiers, leaving only their shadows behind. More than one hundred thousand people had died from fire, wind, and radiation. It was a chilling reminder of the fragility of life.

Some Asian countries have a large number of temples and much idolatrous worship. Dozens of colorful idols and altars can be found on any street. Though surrounded by this intense spiritual darkness, the Christians we encountered were passionately committed to Christ. Their earnestness of prayer deeply touched me. I had never seen prayer meetings quite like this! Whether quietly or with exuberance, everyone prayed simultaneously out loud in the languages of the Holy Spirit. Often with tears, fervent and persistent prayer was offered. Sometimes the meetings lasted for hours.

After returning to Canada for a short time, I continued on an extensive speaking tour through Scandinavia. A friend, Dr. Tony Stone, then arranged services in England and Scotland. A few years later, I also had the privilege of ministering to churches in Northern Ireland. It has been an honor to share the gospel on many occasions across Great Britain, the land of my ancestry.

Amidst all this travel, I was able to tuck in a fascinating eight-day sightseeing trip to Israel. Biblical geography came alive to me as I walked the streets of Jerusalem and rode the waves of Galilee. It was a tremendous and valued experience for which I am grateful.

In 1995, our ministry made several necessary office purchases. Soon my mobile home became overcrowded. The last straw was when the new photocopier wouldn't fit into the office and had to be moved into my living room! We needed more space.

After earnestly seeking the Lord, I was led to a house just down the street. The owner, Lawrence Trafford, had recently moved to Saskatoon. When I enquired, he offered me the house if I would take over the mortgage. It was a miracle of a deal!

With four times the space of the mobile home, we now had ample room for the office as well as my home. The property also had a lovely yard and garden. The Lord had orchestrated an amazing provision.

Fourteen

Eastern Europe

*God's sovereignty does not mean He
orchestrates evil, but rather that He can
bring beauty and restoration out of the
brokenness caused by it.*[7]
Dr. Lucas D. Shallua

As the former Soviet states came out from under communism, they faced challenges adapting to the freedoms we often take for granted. They struggled to evade mafia solicitors while seeking to understand and survive the open market. Both good and bad influences from the West flooded into these nations. It was overwhelming and destabilizing for many people.

---

[7] Lucas D. Shallua, "Sovereignty of God Quotes," *Goodreads*. Date of access: August 8, 2023 (https://www.goodreads.com/quotes/tag/sovereignty-of-god).

During this time, there was unprecedented freedom to preach the gospel in the Eastern Bloc countries. Thousands of people came to know Christ. It was tremendous to witness this incredible response. Believers welcomed me to minister in Romania, Estonia, Latvia, and Ukraine. In some of these countries, people had lived for many years with the terrible tension of legalism and fear under communism. It would take time for them to discover the life and liberty of God's marvelous grace.

When I first arrived in Romania, I got the impression that my presence was creating a dilemma. The pastor who had invited me was a visionary and desired to see many people come to Jesus. However, he faced opposition because their organization wasn't open to women in ministry. Now that I had come, what were they going to do with me? They didn't know how to give me liberty to speak without creating a great deal of friction among those who were very conservative.

One of them discovered that I played the guitar and sang country gospel music—and so, after much debate, they reached a solution. I could begin the service by playing the guitar and singing. Then I could share, as long as I kept holding the guitar.

At the end of my talk, I was to sing again. In this way, they could tell the people that I wasn't actually preaching; I was giving a testimony. Holding the guitar would make all the difference.

It seemed that both men and women were welcome to give a testimony. What amazing theological gymnastics!

Despite the awkwardness and discomfort of holding the guitar while I shared, the Lord worked in the hearts of these precious people. I testified for nearly an hour everywhere I went. The guitar didn't stop the power of the Holy Spirit from working. Folks were saved and healed in every service we held in Romania.

Later I had the opportunity to minister in Estonia, where the people expressed a great openness and hunger for God. Some would walk several kilometers to attend the services. Every night of the week, the churches were filled to capacity. Many responded, seeking prayer for salvation and healing. The people were profoundly grateful for their newfound freedom to worship. Like thirsty sponges, they absorbed the Word of God.

Pastor Eerik Rahkema was one of those who welcomed me warmly into the Baptist Church in Haapsalu, Estonia. He gave me great liberty to preach the gospel and pray for the sick. Whenever I spoke, the altar filled up with people desiring prayer for salvation, restoration, and healing.

Although Estonians seemed to be quite reserved by nature, these friends responded with heartfelt kindness. Many had never seen a free-world Westerner and were overjoyed to welcome me into their homes.

After Estonia, I went into Latvia. When I met the host pastor at the border, he introduced me to the only person in his church who could speak English, a sixteen-year-old lad who was to be my interpreter.

We ate in a roadside restaurant on our way to the service and I began to feel queasy. Following the service, I was quite unwell.

The pastor had arranged for me to stay in a small cottage, with the young interpreter given a room in the same place. Shortly after midnight, I became violently ill. It seemed like I upchucked everything I had eaten for the last week! Despite my pain and discomfort, however, I did count my blessings—there was toilet paper, a very rare commodity in these countries at that time.

I was in agony for five hours while my stomach cleaned itself out. I gloomily wondered if my last will and testament was up to date and how these dear folks would dispose of my body!

As morning came, I felt somewhat better but totally exhausted.

When the interpreter came from his room to make breakfast, he was aghast at the sight of me. I was white as a ghost. He went to get the pastor, who came with his wife.

After prayer, I rapidly began to improve and miraculously was able to preach that afternoon and evening. In fact, I preached often and felt fine the rest of the time I was there. I shall be forever grateful for the kindness of these precious friends.

When I returned to Estonia a few days later, I shared this episode with the woman in whose home I stayed. She informed me that she had heard recent news of twenty-two people ending up in the hospital with food poisoning in a town near to where I had visited. Several of those people had died! I counted my blessings again and praised the Lord for His mercy.

In 2002, Pastor Droz and his wife invited me to join them on a ministry tour through Ukraine. A Ukrainian woman traveled with us to assist along the journey. People stood for hours to get into the auditoriums, even though it was November and cold outside, about -15ºC. It was just as cold inside as outside, however, as there was no indoor heating.

In one of our first services, several thousand people filled the building. At the end of a simple gospel message, I invited those who were ready to surrender to Christ to stand to their feet. The entire crowd stood up!

I turned to the interpreter and told him that they must have misunderstood. I only meant to pray for those who had never before given their hearts to the Lord.

He looked at me incredulously. "But none of these people have ever heard the gospel before. They all want to follow Jesus!"

What a revelation! For the next three weeks, this same experience was repeated nearly everywhere I spoke.

Immediately before the service in one city, a young woman made her way toward me and explained that she had seen me in a dream three weeks earlier. The Lord had spoken, telling her that many people would come to Jesus and be healed in the services. This was a tremendous encouragement and confirmation of the Lord's presence with us.

In another service, a crippled woman came up for prayer. She was in a wheelchair but could walk a little with the help of crutches. When we prayed for her, the power of God instantly touched her. She laid aside her crutches and began to walk, then run around the room. Immediately there was a great release of faith and many others also received healing.

When we visited the city of Lutsk, arrangements were made for our ministry team to stay in an apartment. One evening after the service, I passed the kitchen and saw a rat jump from the counter and disappear down a hole beside the stove. Startled, I shrieked!

We searched for something to fill the hole, then worried that there could be more rodents in the apartment. I was particularly concerned since I was sleeping on a mat on the floor. I was not at all impressed with the idea of free-roving rats!

Thankfully, we didn't find another one.

Fifteen

Exceptional Companions

*There is nothing on this earth more to be
prized than true friendship.*[8]
Thomas Aquinas

While in France in early 1999, a young Belgian named Christelle Colant came to the services where I was speaking. Having completed her Bible school studies, she was now employed in the school's office. She told me that she felt called to evangelism and asked if she could travel with me as an intern.

Several women, as well as a couple of nephews, have accompanied me over the years on short-term missions. Sometimes we've ministered together for a weekend.

---

[8] Isabella Cavallo, "80 Friendship Quotes that Are Meaningful and Heartwarming," April 11, 2023 (https://www.prevention.com/life/a43541874/friendship-quotes).

On other occasions, the arrangement has lasted several months.

My purpose in bringing others alongside me has been, and still is, to enlarge their vision of Christian service and equip them to become leaders in evangelism. It is very important to me that those who participate in ministry understand the sacrifices that are necessary to reach people, and the ultimate joy of bringing them to know Christ. These missions are not pleasure trips but rather opportunities to receive training and serve the assemblies where the Lord leads. Those who traveled with me have enriched my life and impacted the people to whom we've ministered.

Christelle was exceptional. Miraculously healed of epilepsy at the age of nineteen, her vibrant testimony brought faith and healing to many. For more than ten years starting in 1999, she traveled with me as much as possible. She was involved with translating, singing, preaching, and praying. People were touched by her dynamic personality. Together, she and I saw the power of God transform hundreds of lives.

While ministering with me in New Brunswick, she met another young woman who suffered from severe epilepsy. Christelle shared her testimony of healing and then prayed for this woman. We heard later that she was completely healed. She never again experienced an epileptic seizure.

On one occasion, Christelle was horrified to discover a huge hole in her stocking just before we were to go onto the platform to sing.

"No problem," I whispered to her. "You go in front of me and I'll follow close behind. That way no one will see the hole in your stocking."

I followed as close as possible and thus did not see the open guitar case lying across the aisle. As gracious as a swan diving into a mud puddle, I tripped and fell in.

Of course no one noticed her stocking! Everyone watched me as I picked my upended self out of the guitar case.

We once stayed in a beautiful apartment on a farm in Switzerland. While there, she saw a mouse, screeched, and leapt onto a chair. I don't like mice either.

Finally, with help from the owners, we were able to set traps and settle down for the night.

At about one-thirty in the morning, I was awakened from my deep sleep by Christelle pouncing on my bed. Apparently a mouse had been caught in a trap in her room. She woke up to hear the creature squeaking and jumping, trying to escape. Terrified, she'd stepped out of her bed onto a chair. Then, alternating with another stool, she had walked on the chairs to get out of her room.

By the time I went to investigate, the mouse was dead. Poor thing!

We ministered all across Canada, as well as in many other countries on dozens of tours. She also traveled extensively with her own evangelistic ministry. She has been used by the Lord to bring salvation and healing to many.

Later, the Lord opened doors for her to share with another mission organization in an effective outreach throughout Europe. She is now married and continues to serve the Lord in a new season of life as she raises her children.

Another young woman joined me during a European ministry tour in 2008. Laetitia Marq, also from Belgium, had been a professed atheist. However, after a life-changing encounter with Christ she passionately pursued Him. A gifted communicator, she shared her testimony in countless assemblies.

During a very cold spell in January 2009, Laetitia came to be with me in Canada. The temperature that day had dropped to about -45°C, but I suggested that we bundle up and go for a walk.

She was not impressed. When we stepped out into the crisp air, she told me that her face was surely going to crack and fall off!

Her years of living as an atheist, then experiencing the power of God in such a dynamic way, gave her an extraordinary ability to connect with youth. Teenagers and young adults were drawn to her like bees to honey.

She presented the gospel with tremendous skill. Dozens of folk were powerfully impacted by the reality of Christ in her life.

She is married now. With her talented husband and three sons, she is involved in missions in Europe, as well as church-planting in Belgium.

Besides the amazing people who have chosen to join me on my journeys, other companions have also brought great joy and blessing. It has been necessary for trusted people to work behind the scenes while I was away from home for many months at a time.

I am very grateful for the wonderful staff who have faithfully cared for the daily operations of the ministry. Darlene Kienle has managed the office with the capable help of Leanne Simpson and Karen Bashforth. On occasion others have helped as well. They have worked with excellence. It has been a great comfort to know I can contact them in an emergency. Sometimes they've been a listening ear when I was confronted with perplexing issues. They have been willing and available to assist me in any way they can.

The board of Inspiration Ministries is a fantastic group of men and women of integrity. They have challenged me to continually move forward, using every tool available to spread the gospel. Together we are pursuing the vision to touch people with the love of God. I have treasured their prayer support and encouragement.

My mother had a powerful influence in my life and did everything possible to encourage me to fulfill the ministry the Lord has put in my heart. She had a lively sense of humor but was very down-to-earth and practical. She earnestly pursued Christ. Her love, prayer, and example of persevering courage made an enormous impact upon me.

She passed away in 2009 in her ninety-sixth year, six months after the death of my eldest brother, Wesley. I went through a necessary season of grieving, but in these losses the reality of our hope in Christ has brought comfort and courage. Hours before her passing, my mother spoke of the angels she saw surrounding her. With my sister beside her, she slipped quietly away in great peace.

Family members have cheered me on and inspired me as they reassured me of their love and support. Sometimes they are amused, other times irritated by my boisterous temperament. My brother Allan once nicknamed me Hurricane!

My sister Velma and her husband Cory know that I tend to be quite enthusiastic and animated. One Christmas, I received perfume as a gift. I dabbed some on and asked my brother-in-law for his opinion. He did not like it. I tried a second sample. He did not like that one either.

"Neither of those perfumes suit your personality," he explained. "You need one with the smell of burning gunpowder!"

All over the world, I have encountered precious people who have opened their hearts and homes to me. They have offered comfort, encouragement, and friendship. Their prayer and support have renewed my inspiration.

As believers, we work together in the Kingdom of God and encourage one another. The joy we experience as we walk with Jesus increases tremendously when we share the journey with others who know and love Him.

Sixteen

CHALLENGES AND CONFLICTS

*Courage is not simply one of the virtues, but
the form of every virtue at the testing point.*[9]
C.S. Lewis

I have encountered danger, difficulty, and discouragement during my years of itinerant ministry. Working
with different people and cultures can be challenging and
one must learn to adapt quickly to unforeseen, last-minute
changes. Sometimes one's personal preferences have to be
sacrificed. Obstacles may suddenly demand a detour.

Personally, it has been a life-changing revelation
to understand the gift God has given us—the power of
choice. I am today the result of decisions made yesterday.
I will be tomorrow the result of my choices today. I can't

[9] C.S. Lewis, "Courage is not simply…" *BrainyQuote*. Date of access: August 8, 2023 (https://www.brainyquote.com/quotes/c_s_lewis_100842).

always select my circumstances, but I can always choose my attitudes and reactions.

When I passed through moments of discouragement and disappointment, the Lord marvelously sustained me. My heart has been filled with joy in His service. I can't remember a time when I felt like giving up the ministry.

But there have been times when I wondered how I would find the strength and courage to keep going. As I choose to walk on, however, abundant grace is supplied step by step.

Through the years, hundreds of people have offered wonderful hospitality. Wherever I've gone, I have been met with delightful experiences of friendship, fellowship, and good food.

Occasionally I've had unnerving experiences, though. In one instance I was billeted in a home where there were fourteen cats—thirteen too many!

In another city, a pastor asked if I would accompany him and his wife to visit a woman in the community. While there, sitting on the couch, I noticed unusual dusters over the arms of the couch and two reclining chairs. They looked like cat skins. I remarked about their uniqueness.

"Oh yes, I love my cats," the woman replied. "When they die, I have them skinned. I use their hides for furniture dusters in remembrance of them."

What a novel idea!

One time I stayed in the basement of a freshly renovated home. The long descending staircase was covered in lush carpet, ending in a lovely den. Bidding my hosts goodnight, I started downstairs. I'm not exactly sure what happened, but my feet turned into skis when my slippery socks hit that plush carpet. I sailed down the entire flight of stairs, miraculously staying upright as my heels hit every step. Like a slalom racer, I dodged every obstacle before landing at the bottom still on my feet—then slid across the floor until I connected with the wall.

I turned around to see the entire family standing at the top, their eyes as wide as fried eggs.

In unison, the family exclaimed, "Are you all right?" Except for my pride, I was none the worse for the bumpy ride.

I have also been blessed with excellent health. Usually I can eat anything and am able to adapt to different climates and situations quite easily. Most of the food has been great, although I have occasionally experienced food poisoning.

I've also encountered a few exceptionally interesting dishes. For example, I've struggled to eat horse meat, commonly served in some countries. Having spent a great deal of my teenage years in the saddle, I have a psychological block. One shouldn't eat one's friends!

The island of Corsica is a beautiful French province renowned for its exquisite cuisine. When I heard we were going to have quail for supper, I was delighted. The problem was that the quail arrived on my plate with everything except feathers and innards! I did a double take when I saw the head and feet still on the bird. Not particularly used to my food watching me while I eat, I covered its head with a lettuce leaf.

Of course, I've suffered a few embarrassing moments. While preaching in a church in Finland, the message was translated twice: from English to Swedish, then to Finnish. The building was filled with people. The two interpreters and I shared a small platform about thirty centimeters high, covered with a rather tattered rug.

At the end of the service, people crowded around the front for prayer. As I stepped down toward them, the heel of my shoe caught in the carpet. I fell facefirst and landed flat on the floor. I bounced straight up again like a rubber ball, my face flaming with embarrassment.

I turned to see the two interpreters, wide-eyed.

"Are you all right?" they asked simultaneously.

I nodded and kept praying for as many as I could reach. I sincerely hoped very few had seen my nosedive.

After the service, I spoke to an older man who had been standing far at the back of the building. Had he seen me fall?

"Oh yes," he soothingly replied. "Everyone saw you fall, but the presence of the Lord was so powerful that we just assumed you couldn't stand up!"

While ministering at a church in New Brunswick, I was asked to speak to the youth group. I was a little unnerved when I entered the room to about forty loud and boisterous young people between the ages of twelve and twenty. Years earlier I had preached at dozens of youth and teen camps, but now I was older. How would I keep their attention? At the sight of gray hair, they might just tune out.

I panicked momentarily. When I was introduced, I could see their disinterest.

With sudden inspiration, I bounced off my chair, grabbed my electric guitar, and played a jazzy gospel chorus. Instantly I had their full attention. All eyes were glued to me.

Not intending for me to hear, one young fellow with eyes like dinner plates whispered to his friends, "Look, you guys, that old lady plays electric guitar!"

Old lady indeed!

A few encounters could have posed serious danger, but the Lord has protected me and directed my path. I am grateful for His intervention. It has been said that when you're at home sitting in front of your fireplace, you'll wish you could have an adventure. But when you're having an adventure, you'll wish you were at home in front of your fireplace!

One afternoon in a suburb of Paris, a local pastor offered to drive me to the post office on our way to another church across the city. We exited the post office and got into his car. He neglected to lock the doors.

I was holding my wallet on my lap when four young men sauntered in front of the car. Suddenly, two of them jumped to either side of the vehicle and jerked open the doors. Their long, sticky fingers reached in for my wallet. I gripped it as long as I could, struggling to hang on, but it slipped from my grasp. I'm not sure what hit my cheek—the thief's hand, my hand, or the wallet—but I ended up with a shiny black eye.

I jumped out of the car to chase them. Stupid! They were long gone. I knew they wouldn't get much money out of it, but I was very concerned because my passport had been in the wallet.

After filing police reports and medical reports and making calls to cancel credit cards, we went on our way to the evening meeting. The black eye made a notable conversation piece. Despite it all, the Lord gave me grace to minister in the service.

It was a troubling experience, however, and I tossed and turned most of the night, reliving the moment and praying for a solution. Someone had very wisely told me to carry a photocopy of my passport in separate luggage, which thankfully I had done. The next day I took the photocopy to the Canadian embassy to begin the process of getting the passport replaced. What a huge relief it was to get a new passport within two days.

On another occasion, while in Leytonstone, England, I ministered in a church that had once been an old cathedral. It had been completely refurbished and the meeting room held several hundred people. When speaking, I chose to stand in a small space on the floor rather than perch up on the high platform behind me. This placed me right in front of the people sitting in the first row. Two of the leaders, Pastor Mervyn Tilley and his assistant, sat there, one on each side of the aisle.

While I spoke, I saw a young man come into the building carrying a tennis racket. He sat at the back, about fifty meters away, but every few minutes he moved ahead about four rows. I kept preaching, trying to concentrate on my message.

Soon the mysterious man was only two rows from the front.

The ushers at the back of the room seemed quite alarmed, but of course the two pastors up front were oblivious to what was happening directly behind them.

Suddenly, the young man stood up again. As he stepped forward, he lifted the racket as though to swat a fly—except I was in line to be the fly! The ushers came running down the aisle to stop him.

I had the presence of mind to quickly step aside and keep on talking!

When the pastors realized what was happening, they sprang up, took the man firmly by the arms, and led him to a side room where others could assist in quieting him. It turned out that he was on drugs and quite psychotic.

The service continued. We praised the Lord for His grace and power.

Over the years, I have worn out several vehicles while driving millions of kilometers all by myself. The Lord has faithfully watched over me through it all. In fact, my car has become my second home and a wonderful place of prayer.

Only the Lord knows how many accidents have been avoided because of His protection. There have been a number of close calls, especially on icy winter roads. Countless guardian angels have been kept busy, I am sure!

One incident remains vivid in my memory. I was driving in a raging blizzard, a whiteout, with snow blowing across a treacherous slush-covered road. I entered a curve. The sticky slush grabbed my car and pulled it uncontrollably into oncoming traffic.

Suddenly, at the last second, my car swerved and I missed a head-on crash.

People have occasionally asked me about the opposition I've faced being a woman in ministry. I can honestly say that I have had very little difficulty. If a church's leadership doesn't approve, they never invite me. If the leadership wants me to come to their assemblies, they must stand with me. I've never had to fight for an open door. If one door closes, almost immediately several others open.

I've learned that no amount of argument will convince a closed mind. However, I am willing to explain to open-minded folks what God has shown me from His Word on this subject.

Committees spend their energy with discussions and theological debates, which accomplish very little. While the detractors may insist that what I've undertaken cannot be done, God has helped me to do it! He has vindicated me.

I will not waste my time with critics. Every soul that has been saved, healed, delivered, and filled with the Holy Spirit is a witness for His glory.

Besides, if someone receives a love letter, how the postman looks is unimportant. I'm just delivering God's love letter for anyone who will open their heart to Him.

Seventeen

Encouraging Reports

I will bless the Lord at all times; His praise
shall continually be in my mouth. My soul
shall make its boast in the Lord; the humble
shall hear of it and be glad. Oh, magnify
the Lord with me, and let us exalt His name
together. I sought the Lord, and He heard
me, and delivered me from all my fears.
Psalm 34:1–4

We must never underestimate what God is doing. We may not understand His ways, but we can rest assured that He is at work. Our responsibility is to sow the seed, leaving the harvest in His hands.

As you do not know what is the way of the wind,
or how the bones grow in the womb of her who is

with child, so you do not know the works of God who makes everything. In the morning sow your seed, and in the evening do not withhold your hand... (Ecclesiastes 11:5–6)

It often takes years for me to hear of the remarkable things God has done as a result of these services. One assembly in Belgium informed me that because of outreaches we've held there over the years, at least twenty-two people have been added to the church.

Very recently, a man in Switzerland spoke about having met me thirty-two years earlier, drug-addicted and hopeless. Jesus had touched his life. He had left that service saved and sober, completely delivered from drugs.

Siggy Helga related her story to me. In 1994, she had been a nineteen-year-old atheist. A friend had invited her to hear a Canadian woman speaking at a church in Reykjavik, Iceland.

Her first impression was that I was rather outdated and drab. She'd left the meeting to have a cigarette, only to begin coughing uncontrollably. She went back inside to get a drink of water, just in time to hear me say, at the conclusion of the message, "God is calling you."

Somewhat intrigued, she returned to her seat and inexplicably began to cry. She couldn't understand what was happening.

Meanwhile, people were going to the front of the church to give their lives to Christ and have their prayer needs met.

Her friend took her by the shoulders and said, "God is calling you, Siggy. We must go forward for prayer."

As they stood together with dozens of others, I received a word from the Lord and spoke directly to her: "God is healing your ovaries right now!" Her arms shot into the air and she received a jolt of God's power.

At that instant, she was converted to Christ.

Someone gave her a Bible. She left the city the next day for a week-long trip and found that she couldn't stop reading the Word of God. Starting at the book of Job, of all places, she read the entire Bible. When she returned home, she realized that although she had been a chain-smoker she had not touched one cigarette the whole week.

She had been scheduled for surgery two weeks later to remove her ovaries due to a serious medical condition. The doctor had told her she would never have children.

She insisted on having another examination before surgery. To the amazement of everyone, there was no sign of the disease.

While I was on another ministry trip to Iceland more than twenty years later, in 2015, she shared with me the wonders God had done in her life. She was now married with three healthy children.

Hundreds of cards, letters, and emails have brought me great encouragement over the years. I have kept many of them as reminders of God's faithfulness. Folks have shared how their lives have been impacted with changed hearts and restored health.

I received one such letter from a young woman, Michelle. As a rebellious fourteen-year-old, she had been dragged to a small church in Washington by her mother in 1992. Internally kicking and screaming, she had been forced to sit in the service. As I began to speak, however, her attention had been riveted by the humor in my message about Jesus and Peter. She'd thought I was a preacher who doubled as a comedian!

At the end of the message, when I made the call for commitment to Christ, suddenly she stopped laughing. She knew God was calling her. The compulsion of the Holy Spirit to respond was so strong that she could not resist. She knew it was a divine appointment with Christ.

Eleven years later, when she wrote the letter, she and her pastor husband were serving the Lord in a thriving church in Mexico. Having a degree in communications, she was involved in television ministry, broadcasting in more than one hundred countries around the world. Each month, she went into prisons to share the gospel. She wrote to me that while ministering in a juvenile correctional facility, fourteen teenage girls had recently been led to the Lord.

"Thank you for making an altar call in that small Washington church," she concluded in her letter. "Thank you for capturing my attention with your humor... Your obedience has saved my life and given me purpose and destiny... I can go and share the hope you shared with me."

My friend Doreen told me that in early 2023 she visited a ministry center in a small community in Canada's Northwest Territories. While there, she met a French-speaking Swiss man who wrestled with English. However, his whole countenance lit up when he came to understand that she knew me. It was a God-directed encounter in the middle of nowhere!

"Anita Pearce!" he exclaimed. "Yes, I know Anita Pearce. I was fourteen years old when I was baptized in the Holy Spirit in her meetings. It changed my life. My grandfather also received the Holy Spirit at the same time."

A few years ago, a man spoke to me after a service in Lausanne, Switzerland. His mother had been converted in 1980 on my first visit to that church. He commenced to relate to me the title and main points of the sermon! Thirty-five years later, he still remembered my message.

I made a mental note not to preach that sermon in this church again—at least, not for a few more years.

Sometimes the journey is long, the days tiring, and the results seemingly invisible. In one city, for example, I thought little had been accomplished. The response had been tepid, the audience seeming detached and disinterested. I felt disheartened, as if spinning my wheels in deep mud.

Several years later, I returned to that church. A young couple informed me that they had been near divorce at the time of my first visit. They had been lost and without hope. But at the same meeting where I had felt discouraged, they had experienced an encounter with God. Now they were fully engaged in service to Christ.

As I boarded the train to go on to the next place of ministry, I remembered the words of Jesus: *"You did not choose Me, but I chose you and appointed you that you should go and bear fruit, and that your fruit should remain, that whatever you ask the Father in My name He may give you"* (John 15:16). I claim that promise.

Eighteen

MOVING FORWARD

*Through the Lord's mercies we are not
consumed, because His compassions fail not.
They are new every morning; great is Your
faithfulness. "The Lord is my portion," says
my soul, "Therefore I hope in Him!"*
Lamentations 3:22–24

My itinerant ministry has continued full steam ahead as I've crisscrossed Canada, Europe, and many other countries, usually going for four or five months at a time. So far I have made well over one hundred transatlantic flights, averaging two to three hundred services each year. The Lord has been present everywhere I've gone. One or two people here, or dozens of folks over there, have received the touch of the Holy Spirit. It is thrilling to return to various assemblies and hear what God has done.

My journeys have followed a sort of preaching circuit. One spring, for example, I would travel through the west of Canada. The next spring, I would journey to eastern Canada. Each Canadian trip would be followed by a foreign missionary tour in the autumn. And every third year I would travel extensively outside of Canada.

The itinerary has been very flexible, however, dependent on open doors and invitations.

"You need to write a book," several friends have told me. Through the years, I've kept a record of articles, observations, and experiences, some of which I have shared in my newsletters. However, understanding how to publish a book has been a learning curve! Mercifully, the Lord brought several skilled friends and editors to correct and encourage my efforts.

After my first book was written in 2004, another inspiration came, and then another. Several more books have now been published, and their sales have made it possible to increase our mission support.

In 2016, I had a unique opportunity to minister in Nunavut in the Canadian Arctic. It was deeply moving to share with the precious Inuit people.

One evening, dozens received the baptism of the Holy Spirit. An Inuit woman told me that she had heard me clearly speak a phrase in Inuktitut as I prayed in other tongues. Apparently I had said, "The Lord rejoices over you, for you are His precious treasure."

Later that year, I received an invitation to Martinique, a territory of France in the Caribbean. I found a very vibrant group of churches and pastors there who were actively persevering to spread the gospel across the island.

Together with a mission team, I returned to Brazil in 2017. Besides sharing in several churches, it was a highlight to meet some of the children this ministry has sponsored over the years. It brought tremendous joy to know that finances generated by the sale of my music and books have made a difference in providing for them.

In 2020, having just completed three weeks of services in Switzerland at the beginning of a four-month tour through Europe, the world suddenly shut down with the arrival of COVID-19. I was forced to cancel all arrangements and return home.

After the first two months of lockdown, local speaking opportunities opened again. Almost every weekend I was invited to share in assemblies within driving distance of home. I was also involved with music ministry in my home church when possible.

Then I discovered Zoom! Going online, I was able to continue sharing the gospel of hope. It was possible to interact with dozens of groups across Canada and in other countries without even leaving my office.

I thoroughly enjoyed my time during the two years I was forced to stay near home. After forty-one years of constant travel, it was a treat to sleep in the same bed every night.

I was able to complete other projects as well. One of my nephews helped me produce a country gospel Christmas CD, as well as place all my music on music-streaming platforms.

As opportunities and invitations for itinerant ministry continue, the Lord provides the necessary strength, wisdom, and courage. We move forward one day at a time, trusting the Lord to direct the details, knowing that our lives are in His hands.

Barnabas was nicknamed Mr. Encouragement by his colleagues. I was struck by his character, evidenced in Acts 11:23–24: *"When he came and had seen the grace of God, he was glad, and encouraged them all that with purpose of heart they should continue with the Lord... And a great many people were added to the Lord."*

Barnabas's example describes my ministry! On occasion I have been invited to speak to very large audiences of several thousand people. However, most of the time I minister in small assemblies to just a handful of people, sometimes in forgotten corners of the world. My purpose has always been to clearly present the gospel and encourage and inspire people who already know and love

Jesus. The mission statement of Inspiration Ministries is simple: sharing spiritual renewal with evangelistic focus.

We all stand on equal ground before the cross of Christ. One of my treasured Bible verses is 1 John 1:9: *"If we confess our sins, He is faithful and just to forgive us our sins and to cleanse us from all unrighteousness."* The precious blood of Jesus Christ washes our hearts by faith, giving us hope and redemption while we walk on with Him. As we increasingly yield our hearts and wills to Christ, the Holy Spirit continually keeps the passion to love and serve Him ablaze within us.

As a result of reading these testimonies of God's faithfulness to me, it is my prayer that you will pursue Christ with renewed fervor and courage. Keep following Jesus one day at a time. Diligently study the Word of God. Trust God. Obey Him. Let God use you to bless the people He has placed around you. Never give up. Run the race with joy.

CONCLUSION

The snow gently fell as I drove into town. After the four-hour journey, I was tired. I turned into a drive-thru and picked up a hamburger. Coffee would help perk me up!

When I arrived at the church, someone was already there. I immediately started unloading the van and setting up the book table. I set up my guitar and portable sound system. I did a sound check. Several folks gathered early for prayer.

Although only about twenty people had braved the cold evening, the worship team sang with all their hearts. As I ministered, the folks were very attentive.

I noticed a young man who seemed especially moved when I spoke of God's willingness to give us a second chance despite our failures and sin.

At the end of the message, I invited anyone who desired prayer to come forward. This young man stepped out of his place, brushing tears away. He longed for a restoration of his relationship with the Lord. Together with the pastor, we prayed with him.

Others had responded with various needs as well. An older woman was in distress because of a family crisis. A middle-aged man had just lost his job. We prayed, trusting God to intervene for each one.

After the service, several people expressed appreciation for what the Lord had done in bringing encouragement, salvation, and renewal. Two or three gentlemen assisted me as I packed up the book table, putting everything back in the vehicle. It had been a typical gospel meeting.

I reflected on the service as I drove to the home where I would stay. This is what I do. I travel from place to place, singing and preaching. Some folks come to Jesus for salvation, some receive healing, and some are baptized in the Holy Spirit; hopefully everyone is encouraged in their walk with God. Most of the time I have no idea what has really happened in their hearts.

As an itinerant evangelist, I have had a few moments of popularity, even notoriety! Some may think itinerant ministry to be romantic or glamourous. After long and tiring journeys, unpleasant circumstances, or difficult people, however, the romance can wear rather thin. Often the power of the Holy Spirit is poured out in ordinary ways and seemingly insignificant places, not for glamour but for the glory of God.

My responsibility is to trust and obey the Lord. Jesus said in Luke 9:23–24,

> If anyone desires to come after Me, let him deny himself, and take up his cross daily, and follow Me. For whoever desires to save his life will lose it, but whoever loses his life for My sake will save it.

Only eternity will reveal what God has done. He has been forever faithful.

The divine pursuit which captures my soul is an unfolding discovery of God's love. All His works are but a fleeting glimpse of the grandeur of *who He is*. Knowing Christ far supersedes all that He has done.

I share Paul's earnest desire when he wrote in Philippians 3:10, *"...that I may know Him..."* And so, I passionately pursue Christ.

> Through many dangers, toils and snares,
> I have already come;
> 'Tis grace has brought me safe thus far,
> And grace will lead me home.[10]

---

[10] John Newton, "Amazing Grace," 1779.

The Gift of Salvation

If you have never given your life to Christ, I earnestly urge you to surrender to Him today. According to Romans 3:23, *"all have sinned and fall short of the glory of God."*

The Bible tells us that peace with God is received by turning to Him from our sins:

> ...if you confess with your mouth the Lord Jesus and believe in your heart that God has raised Him from the dead, you will be saved. For with the heart one believes unto righteousness, and with the mouth confession is made unto salvation... For "whoever calls on the name of the Lord shall be saved." (Romans 10:9–10, 13)

You can receive His life now by repentance and faith. Pray this simple prayer:

Lord, I know I have sinned. I believe You are the Son of God and that You died on the cross to forgive my sins. I believe You have risen from the dead with power to give me a transformed life. Please forgive me, change my heart, and set me free. I surrender the control of my will to You. Help me to follow You. In Jesus's name, amen.

Read the Bible and pray every day. Find others who love Jesus and can help you to follow Him. Jesus will lift you from the darkness of sin; He will set you on a solid rock and fill your heart with a new song of praise. Let Him be the center of your life.

ALSO BY ANITA PEARCE

ISBN: 978-0-9783781-0-3

Our character and core values are results of our choices. We have the tremendous capacity to determine who we will be. We cannot always control our circumstances, but we do have power to decide our reactions and attitudes in response to them. It is that ability which enables us not just to survive, but also to thrive in seemingly impossible situations—to turn lemons into lemonade. This book presents the challenge to choose to follow Christ and live life passionately.

ISBN: 978-1-4866-0146-2

Thoughts are powerful. When we take personal responsibility for our thoughts and their consequences, we can reject destructive patterns. Replacing them with quality values brings order to our inner world. As we submit to Jesus Christ through the Word of God, the dynamics of Holy-Spirit-controlled thinking produces profound transformation in our minds. This book challenges us that we can always choose to change the way we think—and experience a renewed mind.

ISBN: 978-1-4866-1416-5

Contentment is a choice. Although we face constant pressure to be someone we're not, and to desire more than we have, it is our responsibility to refuse discontentment. This book reveals the keys that can unlock serenity, the source of which is a living, personal relationship with Jesus Christ.

Choose a Contented Heart will challenge you to apply principles which produce profound peace and satisfaction from His life within you.

ISBN: 978-1-4866-1773-9

Shadows may fall across the path of life, causing distress, dismay, and doubt. Trouble-filled dark experiences may seem stark and hopeless. Yet the Word of God brings the certainty that God's Almighty Hand is always in control. His unfailing presence and promises can restore the song in the midnight of the soul.

Drawn from personal observations and adventures, this compilation of both amusing and serious reflections endeavors to inspire and challenge you to trust the unfailing God.

ADDITIONAL RESOURCES FROM INSPIRATION MINISTRIES

Books:
Above the Storm
Joy in the Journey

Music CDs
Collection of Favorites
Collection of Favorites #2
The Timeless Prize

For a complete catalogue of Anita's music, CDs, DVDs, and other ministry information please visit her website at www.inspirationministries.net.